IN THE
COMMON
INTEREST

Embracing the
New American Community

JOHN CARONA

EMERALD
BOOK CO.

Published by Emerald Book Company
Austin, TX
www.emeraldbookcompany.com

Distributed by Emerald Book Company

For ordering information or special discounts for bulk purchases, please contact Emerald Book Company at PO Box 91869, Austin, TX 78709, 512.891.6100.

Design, cover design, and composition by Greenleaf Book Group LLC
Cover images: ©iStockphoto.com/IP Galanternik D.U. (background) and Monkey Business Images, 2013/Used under license from Shutterstock.com (couple). Interior image page 110: ©iStockphoto.com/pialhovik.

Cataloging-in-Publication data
(Prepared by The Donohue Group, Inc.)
Carona, John.
    In the common interest : embracing the new American community / John Carona.—1st ed.
    p. ; cm.
    Issued also as an ebook.
    Includes bibliographical references.
    ISBN: 978-1-937110-55-0
    1. Common interest ownership community associations—United States. 2. Community life—United States. 3. Home ownership—United States. I. Title. II. Title: Common interest
    HD7287.82.U6 C37 2014
    643/.2/0973   2013940340

Part of the Tree Neutral® program, which offsets the number of trees consumed in the production and printing of this book by taking proactive steps, such as planting trees in direct proportion to the number of trees used: www.treeneutral.com

TreeNeutral®

Printed in the United States of America on acid-free paper

14 15 16 17 18 19   10 9 8 7 6 5 4 3 2

First Edition

Dedicated to the devoted employees of Associa,
who have collectively built our company, brick by brick.

CONTENTS

INTRODUCTION

It's so hard to get on the right wavelength, but I will find a way
to reach my neighbor soon. I'm not sure how much we have in
common, but it's everybody's moon. Shine on, everybody's moon!

—HOWARD ASHBY KRANZ
Songwriter, Everybody's Moon

━━━━━━━━━━━━━━━━━━━━━━━━━━━━

In a nation that embraces the spirit of rugged individualism and
self-reliance, the emergence of community associations as a dominant form of housing may seem anachronistic to some. After all, the
descendants of immigrants who came to America, often with only the
clothes on their backs, searching for a better life and personal freedoms, choose to live in community associations. To the unfamiliar,
these communities may seem to restrict the very freedoms immigrant
ancestors held so dear. What could be at the root of this foundational
change in the American community?

The answer is clear: It is in their common interest. Howard Ashby
Kranz captures the spirit of living in a community that is managed
by an association: neighbors reaching out to each other, searching
for their commonalities—for their mutual interest. Regardless of
their varying degrees of diversity in background and tastes, neighbors are likely to share common experiences, interests, and needs.
Living in peace and harmony and communicating effectively about
shared needs and interests in community associations clearly is to
their advantage.

This emotional equity enhances the primary benefit offered by community associations: protecting and enhancing property values. Homeowners who share these common interests embrace the new American community.

EMBRACING THE
NEW AMERICAN COMMUNITY

The growth of the community association industry as a result of the popularity and affordability of the lifestyle and the benefits to members, developers, and municipalities is undeniable. In the beginning of the community association movement, however, many communities were designed by inexperienced developers and attorneys, including some who seemed intent on limiting both personal expression and freedom of their members. In fact, much of the negative press coverage and some scholarly works about community associations are rooted in communities with governing documents and restrictions dating back to that period.

The modern American community association, however, is a completely different entity. Generally, it is designed and operated to maintain and protect the value of the homes within and to provide amenities and a lifestyle that is mutually beneficial to all members. Simultaneously, it has enabled millions of individuals and families to afford homes and lifestyles that otherwise might have been impossible, expensive dreams.

Certainly this "new American community" has experienced its growing pains and its resultant critics. The proliferation of community associations, however, is a testament to their affordability and mutual benefits for homeowners and municipalities. They are the most attractive housing choice for millions of persons in a wide variety of markets. What's more, they are a boon to local governments, especially to those whose financial limitations affect their ability to improve neighborhoods. That is why they are embraced throughout the United States and, increasingly, throughout the world.

IN THE COMMON INTEREST

In the Common Interest: Embracing the New American Community primarily addresses the phenomenal growth of community associations in the United States and how this lifestyle can be improved to benefit not only residents and their families but also communities and our country. It is intended as an introduction for anyone considering living in an association and as an overview for those who will govern or are governed in one. To further understanding, it explores the elements of community association growth; the operations, benefits, strengths, and weaknesses of this type of housing; the major areas in which to improve community associations; and the outlook for the future of community associations in the United States and around the world.

Issues and chapters

These issues are addressed in interrelated and complementary chapters that are organized into three parts: I. Understanding Community Associations, II. Improving Community Associations, and III. Forecasting Community Associations. Each part includes three chapters, and their focus is summarized in the book's conclusion.

The first chapter of Part I explains how community associations work, while the second focuses on why people are drawn to them, prefer them, and support them. Chapter 3 highlights why they work and will continue to operate.

Chapters 4–6 in Part II offer recommendations for improving community associations through education, performance, and adaptation to external forces.

Building on this foundation, chapters 7–9 in Part III forecast the future of community associations. They focus on how these associations will grow in other parts of the world and how they will adapt to our country's changing demographics and aging population.

Each chapter concludes with a related episode in the life of David and Sandra, a fictional couple typical of those who choose community association living, as well as a section of Frequently Asked Questions.

David and Sandra

Beginning in this introduction and ending in the chapter on aging, the reader will follow the experiences of David and Sandra in addressing myths about community association living. As they move through the stages of their married life, their needs and interests will evolve. Throughout their lives, however, they pursue their version of the American Dream in different but always suitable community associations.

Terminology

Although the terms "community association," "community," and "association" are used interchangeably herein, other equally acceptable terms include "homeowners association" and "planned unit development." Homes in community associations often are referred to as "units," and their buyers are called "homeowners" as often as "members." The latter refers to their automatic membership in the association and differentiates them from renters who may live in the community but are not members.

Author's perspective

This book is written from my perspective as president and CEO of an international realty management firm who is equally passionate about public service and political science. It is my best effort to examine fairly, frankly, and honestly an industry that often is discussed in the public arena. What's more, it is an objective attempt to focus on homeowners and association board members while defining the industry's core values, vision, mission, services, and strategies to improve the quality of life within their boundaries.

Although research based, this book is reader friendly rather than textbook scholarly. Equally important, it is an informal presentation bolstered by my insight gained from more than thirty years of practical experience in the field and by the results of countless observations of diverse scenarios, dialogues, and interactions with leading experts at the local, state, and national levels.

SUMMARY

The American dream of owning a home often is considered a hallmark of success. It often evolves as homeowners' needs change and as they build financial and emotional equity in their residences and neighborhoods of choice. Those who embrace the belief that "my home is my castle" increasingly express related expectations of manicured lawns, attractive neighborhoods, and access to facilities such as swimming pools, parks, and activity centers. Simultaneously, however, many want to spend more time pursuing personal and professional interests and less time maintaining amenities. For them and countless others, the community association lifestyle is the perfect choice.

Buying a home in a community association is especially appealing to those who want more for their money while enjoying a better quality of life—but with fewer obligations. It enables homeowners to maximize their property values and to live in peace and harmony, largely through the leadership of the volunteers they elect from their own ranks to serve on their board of directors.

To accomplish this most efficiently and cost effectively, most boards hire community managers who have the expertise to run the day-to-day operations consistent with their standards and resources. Through their leadership and advice, these professionals empower board members with the knowledge needed to do a better job. Together they deserve much of the credit for the popularity of the community association lifestyle in the United States and beyond.

I have been fortunate to witness the growing demand for community associations and the resultant rapid growth in their numbers. Through *In the Common Interest: Embracing the New American Community* I hope to share some of the very positive benefits that community association members enjoy and to analyze the almost universal appeal of this type of new American community.

This goal should be realized through chapters that focus on how community associations work; why they are so popular; why they will continue to operate; and how we can improve them through education, performance, and adaptation to external forces. The emphasis then turns to the future in chapters focusing on the worldwide growth of this housing phenomenon and how it will adapt to the changing demographics and aging population. Most important, I hope to offer my perspective about how we can build upon a strong foundation to make things even better.

DAVID AND SANDRA
bust myths about community association living

David and Sandra are a young married couple who are eager to purchase their first home. Because their careers keep them busy and children are only a twinkle in their eyes, they are considering buying a condominium instead of a single-family home. Neither wants the hassles or upkeep associated with a house, and both believe strongly that building financial equity *must start now*. Renting is behind them.

Because they want to spend more time enjoying amenities such as pools and clubhouses and less time doing maintenance chores,

David and Sandra are interested in living in a community managed by an association. While they understand the conveniences of doing so, they also have heard some criticism. Their question is simple: Are these criticisms warranted, or are they myths that can be busted? The answer will be revealed in the chapters that follow as we share the experiences of this young couple as their family grows and their needs and interests evolve through the years.

PART I

UNDERSTANDING COMMUNITY ASSOCIATIONS

CHAPTER 1

How Community Associations Work

A man's house is his castle and fortress,
and each man's home is his safest refuge.

—SIR EDWARD COKE
English jurist, Member of Parliament, and writer

INTRODUCTION

Based on an old English proverb, these words by Sir Edward Coke reinforce the emotional security or equity that is associated with homeownership. The need for individual privacy and safety that they memorialize, however, often is extended to the community in which a home exists. Communities governed by associations often are considered the safest havens, for homeowners choose to live by mutually beneficial rules that enhance not only their emotional security but also their financial investment.

Because homes often are the largest asset in the average homeowner's portfolio, homeowners welcome opportunities to protect and to enhance their safety standards and property values. Many recognize they cannot accomplish this alone, for surrounding properties impact theirs—and vice versa. When they understand how community associations work, they also understand their mutual benefits. The very nature of how and for whom community associations work is responsible for their growth. That is the focus of this chapter and of this book.

ANALYZING THE GROWTH
OF COMMUNITY ASSOCIATIONS

Clearly, community associations are the fastest-growing segment of the housing market in most major cities in the United States. The Community Associations Institute (CAI) reports that in 1970 approximately 2.1 million residents lived in 701,000 units in 10,000 communities managed by associations. By 2011 these numbers rose to 62.3 million residents in 25.1 million units in 314,200 communities. Those two years are bookends to the equally astounding incremental growth that is documented in the table that follows. The table is cited throughout this book, and its figures are expanded differently each time to reinforce varied points.

Estimated number of U.S. association-governed communities and individual housing units and residents within those communities:

Year	Communities	Housing Units	Residents
1970	10,000	701,000	2.1 million
1980	36,000	3.6 million	9.6 million
1990	130,000	11.6 million	29.6 million
2000	222,500	17.8 million	45.2 million
2002	240,000	19.2 million	48.0 million
2004	260,000	20.8 million	51.8 million
2006	286,000	23.1 million	57.0 million
2008	300,800	24.1 million	59.5 million
2010	309,600	24.8 million	62.0 million
2011	314,200	25.1 million	62.3 million

Table 1 - CAI Association Growth Statistics

The growth in the number of community associations reflects more than simply their popularity among home buyers. It underscores their importance to the developers and builders who create them and to the municipalities that often require them and always benefit from them. All three groups derive benefits from them, just as they have responsibilities toward them.

Benefits for homeowners

Homeowners have a choice. One is to live in a community association with a board of directors comprising elected volunteers who strive to protect members' property values while improving their quality of life. Another is to live in a neighborhood comprising independent households without an organization dedicated to pursuing those goals.

In independent neighborhoods, homeowners have to fend for themselves. In associations, however, they can turn to managers to help them cope with a wide variety of issues.

The manager of an association that attracts highly educated homeowners, for example, resolved a concern before it erupted into a feud. One of the residents apparently was growing corn and other crops in the landscaped common area. Even worse, the same resident was catching squirrels, skinning them, and hanging them to dry on coat hangers. The goal? To make squirrel jerky!

Instead of confronting the neighbor, the homeowner called the manager, who intervened immediately. All it took was a letter to the would-be farmer and a complaint filed with the local health department. The situation was resolved without a neighborhood feud.

The educated buyer who comparison shops soon realizes that community associations typically offer a better way of life without many of the maintenance responsibilities associated with non-community association living. What's more, through community associations, developers offer amenity packages that are not achievable by homeowners on their own and provide a higher standard of services than municipalities could.

Benefits for developers

To understand the popularity of the community association lifestyle, it also is essential to consider their appeal to developers of community associations and to the municipalities in which they are created. After all, the CAI data indicating that consumers embrace community associations also indicate that they work for developers and municipalities—or they wouldn't exist.

Great economic incentives can motivate developers to build and sell high-density housing rather than one-of-a-kind single-family homes. Economies of scale enable them not only to use a handful of designs that appeal to a broad target market segment but also to provide amenities that the targeted homeowner otherwise could not afford. Developed to appeal to the targeted market, these can range from pools and clubhouses to parks, playgrounds, fitness centers, tennis courts, and golf courses.

By building a high-density community, a developer can advertise one property that includes all designs at a specific location, instead of the more expensive alternative of creating different campaigns for unique single-family homes at different locations. Many developers enhance their cost-effectiveness by establishing a centralized sales office with a staff that usually works on-site for slightly smaller commissions than independent sales agents and brokers.

Builders outside community associations typically sell unique single-family homes independently or through real estate brokers. There is no economy of scale possible for those who choose this process.

This comparison of cost-effectiveness within and beyond community associations is considered the single most important reason that builders are drawn to association-governed communities.

Benefits for municipalities

Municipalities also benefit from high-density community association housing by maximizing tax revenue per acre of land. Each housing unit, whether a condominium or single-family residence, is taxed separately. If a one hundred–unit condominium is built on a parcel, for example, all one hundred condominiums are taxed individually, as opposed to a one hundred–unit apartment building that would be taxed only as a single commercial property.

Another important benefit to municipalities is the transfer of responsibilities for developing and maintaining infrastructure for the community association. Instead of the municipality spending money and human resources to design, create, and maintain roads, water, sewer, landscaping, and lighting systems, those costs are transferred to the association developer and members. Interestingly, many times the community association will adopt higher maintenance and aesthetic standards than the municipality. Its doing so directly benefits the members and indirectly benefits the larger municipal community by protecting or even enhancing property values.

It seems clear that the benefits to municipalities created an incentive to encourage the growth of community associations. The market responded to these opportunities with a win/win mentality that placed the dream of homeownership within reach for many who otherwise might have been excluded due to the price of entry.

As municipalities experienced the success of the association lifestyle, they encouraged a wider diversity of developments that eventually would cater to every economic stratum. They joined homeowners in embracing associations ranging from affordable housing units to the most luxurious high-rise condominiums; from the small four-unit inner city condominium conversion to the largest-scale community associations like Reston, Virginia, or Sunriver, Oregon; and from active adult to assisted-living retirement communities.

As the industry continues to mature, municipalities, members, and community managers become increasingly knowledgeable and sophisticated about their interrelated opportunities and responsibilities. The lessons they learn strengthen the services and benefits received by all.

DEFINING COMMUNITY ASSOCIATIONS

A community association generally is defined as a nonprofit mutual benefit corporation or an unincorporated organization created to manage the common interests of a community and its residents. Sometimes called a homeowners association (HOA) or a common interest development, it can be a condominium, a planned-unit development, a townhome-style development, or a stock cooperative. Each type of association has a unique ownership structure, and they all offer ways for owners to participate in the operation of the community.

Although terms such as "community association," "community interest development," "homeowners association," "planned unit development," and "property owners association" often are used interchangeably, "community association" is the most generic and encompassing. As used herein it refers to almost any type of association except stock cooperatives.

Most community associations in the United States are nonprofit corporations established under their respective state laws when their developers file Articles of Incorporation with their respective secretaries of state. Other documents include bylaws and a Declaration of Covenants, Conditions, and Restrictions (CC&Rs). Taken together, these are called the "governing documents" and are the road map the members use to operate the association, maintain and insure the common area, and govern the association. Most states also have community association–specific laws that members rely on for guidance.

Types of associations

The governing documents offer guidelines for neighborly collaboration toward the "greater good," whether living in a condominium, a planned unit development, or a stock cooperative. As evident from the definitions below, these property types differ dramatically:

Condominium.

A condominium often is defined as almost any cube in space, whether in a residential building, commercial complex, garage, or even boat dock. Buying a condominium generally means buying a unit defined as existing from the unfinished interior surfaces of the unit inward. This means ownership of the sheetrock and paint but not the studs in the walls.

Condominiums can be high-rise, mid-rise, or low-rise multiunit dwellings, or they can resemble row houses or townhome-style buildings. Although some states define townhomes as a property type, those that have adopted updated laws and property definitions usually include townhome-style properties as condominiums. Their rationale is that the units often share a common wall and that the roofs, land, amenities, and infrastructure are owned in undivided interest by the members. Each member owns an undivided percentage of interest in these items, and the association is responsible for maintaining them. In other words, the association does not hold a separate deed for these items. They are considered a "common area."

Planned unit development.

Planned unit developments (PUD) usually comprise clusters of single-family homes, whether tract or custom, whose owners share parks, pools, and other amenities. Some are mixed-use developments that include commercial, high-rise, townhouse-style, low-rise, or garden condominiums; single-family homes; stock cooperatives; shopping areas; schools; public safety buildings; and even places of worship and libraries.

A PUD can create multiple or subassociations for each type of property within its boundaries. If so, each typically has its own board of directors and sends representatives to the board of their master association.

In a PUD the association can have a deed for the common area, or members can hold an undivided percentage of interest in it. The land the member owns will include mineral, water, and air rights directly below and above it.

Although there are many variations of this type of ownership, the definition above is prevalent.

Stock cooperative.

In a stock cooperative the corporation owns every part of the property, including the living units, building interiors and exteriors, and the land. Rather than purchasing and receiving title to real estate, buyers purchase "stock shares" that entitle them to occupy a unit in the cooperative under the terms of a proprietary lease. In other words, people who live in a stock cooperative lease the units from the co-op by owning shares in it.

Co-ops are operated by boards of directors that are elected by the shareholders (members) of the cooperative—exactly like other community association boards are elected. Cooperative boards, however, arguably may have broader powers than other association boards. The board of a housing cooperative, for example, may judge the potential purchaser's financial stability, character, lifestyle, etc., and investigate his or her criminal history.

Applying to purchase shares in a housing cooperative often is compared to applying for an apartment in a very exclusive apartment building or applying for a highly sought executive position in a large, successful company.

Diverse choices.

These definitions underscore an incredibly rich diversity of community associations that can accommodate almost anyone's lifestyle. Choices will depend on the buyer's preferences, priorities, and limitations regarding countless variables that include the following:

> budget

> neighborhood

> age

> size of family

> › space needs

> › yard maintenance

> › lifestyle

> › social atmosphere and

> › hobbies.

A wealthy retired person who enjoys golf, walking in the woods, and quiet evenings, for example, would choose a totally different community than would a young working couple with activity-driven children and with limited time and resources.

Finding the perfect community and enjoying the benefits of an association can be motivations to improve and strengthen it. This often is accomplished by serving on association committees or on the board of directors. Regardless of the extent of participating, all members benefit from understanding how the association works.

Characteristics of associations

Community associations may vary significantly, but they have three common characteristics that bind members and associations: mandatory membership, mutually binding documents, and lien-based assessments. These should be understood clearly by home buyers because they are cornerstones of success in maintaining and enhancing property values while improving quality of life.

Mandatory membership.
The first characteristic of a community association is mandatory membership, which means that membership is automatic and occurs when anyone becomes an owner of a home in a community association. There is no box to check at settlement to become a member. It happens automatically and is required for home ownership.

Mutually binding documents.
The second characteristic is mutually binding documents that bind

the owner to the association and the association to the owner. These governing documents outline the requirements and responsibilities of both parties. They typically include the association's Articles of Incorporation, CC&Rs, and bylaws. Cumulatively, they are the road map that members use to operate their association, maintain and insure the common area, and govern the association.

Lien-based assessments.
The third characteristic is lien-based assessments. The assessments paid by homeowners to the association pay the costs of maintaining and operating the community. In many cases, by purchasing a home in a community association, an owner agrees to an automatic lien on the property, which authorizes the association to claim his or her home/unit/lot for failure to pay valid fees and charges to the association. In other cases the association is authorized to file a lien for delinquent assessment amounts. In all cases these liens may be enforced through foreclosure by the association.

The three characteristics of community associations are the cornerstone of the interrelationship among homeowners, board members, and management companies. While the homeowners elect the board members who volunteer their time and energy to serve them, the board members can employ management companies that have the resources and expertise to perform their day-to-day operations. Accountability is essential: The board answers to the homeowners, while a management company has a contract with the corporation and is accountable to the board.

UNDERSTANDING PURPOSES OF COMMUNITY ASSOCIATIONS

Perhaps community associations are appreciated most for protecting, maintaining, and enhancing their community's property values. That focus is the foundation of their three main purposes:

> to operate as a business,

> to act as a government, and

> to promote community spirit.

Because community associations typically are multimillion-dollar operations (based on the values of their homes), the board members who govern them must reflect fair, honest, businesslike, democratic principles and practices. They must be fiscally responsible, transparent, accessible, and accountable to homeowners at all times.

Simultaneously, they must recognize that promoting community spirit is as important a purpose as operating as a business or acting as a government. After all, the concept of protecting and increasing property values, while important to any homeowner, is only a portion of the reasons community associations have increased in popularity.

The emotional equity derived from living in a secure environment, having neighbors with common interests and values, and being able to make the community association fit the needs of its homeowners is at least as important as dollar values. Community associations that achieve this emotional equity are in higher demand, and, subsequently, tend to produce higher property values. When home values decline nationally or regionally, preserving emotional equity makes the community association viable.

COEXISTING WITH LOCAL GOVERNMENTS

Community associations coexist successfully with and benefit local governments, despite the dire predictions in some critical studies of associations. Based largely on research performed in the 1980s and 1990s, some critics wrongly warned that community associations rapidly would supplant the roles and services ordinarily provided by local government. Instead, for the most part, community associations offer a higher standard of service in their areas than would be possible if paid by the municipality.

There are many associations whose sole common elements are an entry sign and a small greenbelt. PUDs, sometimes referred to as HOAs, however, maintain their own streets, water system infrastructures, parks, pools, lighting, landscaping, waste removal, and other amenities for the benefit of their members. Some argue that this creates a double-taxation issue for members. If so, it is not to their detriment. The higher standard of care adopted by most community associations often raises the value of properties in the surrounding community and helps keep property tax rates lower than they would be if the association did not exist.

Another unsubstantiated concern was that community associations would form a powerful voting bloc to supplant local government. Although organized efforts to mobilize association members into public voting blocs have been discussed and attempted for years, for the most part they have been unsuccessful. The topic persists because, with the exception of seniors, members of community associations could be the single largest identifiable voting bloc in the United States.

What defies organizational efforts, however, is the inability to identify a common political theme that would unite and mobilize them. The diversity of ages, incomes, and conflicting personal and political priorities is a major impediment to organizing association members around any specific candidate or issue.

Although, ostensibly, the impressive number of associations could form a powerful bloc, either at the local, state, or national levels, that is as unlikely as it is unrealistic. Their number may be impressive, but there is no evidence of association members ever voting as a bloc or of any efforts to organize them into one.

This does not mean, however, that associations shun advocacy. Unlike the early days of association development, today's community associations can choose from a variety of trade associations that vie for them. The national CAI, for example, has chapters in virtually every state. Other local and state trade associations exist as well, and most have legislative monitoring or lobbying arms to help influence legislation affecting associations. They have no history or apparent interest, however, in participating in or being major contributors to political campaigns at any level. Neither have they tapped the potential voting power of the members of their community association constituents for any purpose.

Contrary to some popular assumptions, most community associations and their members never interact with local governments beyond tax and building permit issues. There are exceptions, of course, especially for large-scale communities such as Reston in Virginia and Woodbridge Village in California, where the size of the communities alone dictates a close and coordinated relationship with municipal and even county governments.

As community associations evolved over the years, the relationship between local governments and community associations evolved as well. Whether large or small, community associations act as an adjunct to local governments and are subject to all local laws and ordinances. They are complementary rather than threatening to municipalities in countless ways.

Municipalities, for example, benefit from a concentration of taxable properties that can be achieved no other way. They also enjoy not needing to maintain the infrastructure elements of the community association, such as lighting, water and sewer systems, roads, parks, pools, and other amenities. Since these elements strictly are for their members and guests, community associations are responsible for their standards of maintenance and the cost of their upkeep and replacement. Many times those maintenance standards are higher than the municipality's.

The result is that community associations offer a sense of community and opportunities for an enhanced quality of life. This is accomplished by providing better care of common property than otherwise would be provided by the municipality and by the increase in free time created by assuming responsibility for many basic property maintenance chores.

UNDERSTANDING HOW
COMMUNITY ASSOCIATIONS WORK

Every community association is a mandatory membership association. Its affairs are governed and operated by a board of directors comprising association members who are elected by the membership to serve staggered terms. The advantage of staggering the terms is that not all board members will stand for election every year. Instead, typically one-third of them will be elected each year, meaning that at least two-thirds of the directors will be experienced. This ensures at least a minimal level of leadership continuity for the corporation.

Board members are volunteers, and any member of the community association is eligible to run for a position. In some rare cases the governing documents of the association may stipulate that nonmembers may run as well. An association's success is enhanced when its board members are thoroughly knowledgeable about not only their governing documents but also relevant state laws.

All community associations and their governing documents must comply with local ordinances and with state and federal laws. When there is a conflict, the higher authority prevails. While their laws will differ, most states define community associations as "mutual benefit" corporations, meaning that the associations exist for the mutual benefit of all members. Their responsibilities are defined by their purposes of operating as a business, acting as a government, and promoting community spirit. This means that the board is charged with operating the property in a way that will help protect property values by maintaining and protecting the "bricks and sticks" and curb appeal while creating and enhancing a pleasant place to live.

To be able to pay for property upkeep and administrative costs, community associations levy annual assessments paid by the members in regular intervals. The amounts of the assessments are determined annually by the board and are based on projected annual expenses for maintaining the common area and for other ancillary costs such as utilities, garbage collection, bookkeeping, property insurance, and management fees. The size of the association budget could run from a few tens of thousands to millions of dollars, depending on the size and nature of the community.

To understand the magnitude of governing a community association, suppose an association has two hundred units or homes with an average value of $300,000. Multiplying $300,000 × 200 homes results in $60 million in real estate values. Conservatively, this would require an annual operating budget of $400,000 and a capital replacement reserve of $500,000.

This means the board of directors of that association operates a nonprofit corporation whose assets are approximately $61 million. Board officers and members are charged with the responsibility to "maintain, protect, and enhance" those assets for the benefit of the members by maintaining the structural and aesthetic integrity of the common areas, the curb appeal of the property, the protection of the reserve funds, and a strong sense of community. All these things are designed to protect the resale value of the homes, and the board is responsible for all of them.

The sheer complexity of this responsibility for volunteers often results in the board hiring a community association management company, which, in turn, provides community managers. These professionals have the expertise and support needed to assist and advise board members about the complex laws and responsibilities of running their multimillion-dollar nonprofit corporation. Board members maintain their administrative responsibility but delegate day-to-day operations to those who work under their directives.

FOSTERING TRANSPARENT GOVERNANCE

One criticism leveled at community associations over the years is that boards are small dictatorships whose members unreasonably enforce the rules and restrictions found in the CC&Rs. While history reflects a small number of cases for which this criticism applies, the problem almost always is a temporary matter resolved by the community association method of governance and the election cycles of board members.

The annual election cycle is a democratic process that provides opportunities for any interested members of the association to stand for election. Those elected will be fortunate to join the many members who enjoy contributing to their communities and serving the interests of their neighbors during many successful and fulfilling years on the board.

In the exceptionally rare circumstance of a board member's behavior being illegal or so egregious that it threatens the association or its members, he or she can be removed from the board by an appropriate process and vote of the members. Removal processes likely are detailed in the association's bylaws. This unusual circumstance generally is avoided due to the election cycles and transparency of association governance.

Elections to fill expired terms usually are the highlight of a community association's annual membership meeting. Although most community associations rely on nominating committees to make recommendations to the voting members, many also allow write-in candidates or nominations from the floor. Any association member in good standing can volunteer or be nominated to serve on the board of directors.

At a recent board seminar a particularly disgruntled and agitated homeowner complained that the annual election system should be replaced because it didn't work. When asked why he thought this was the case, he said he knew the system didn't work because he was on the ballot every year and never got elected. Apparently he was ignoring reality: Every year he ran, and every year the membership rejected his candidacy. Unfortunately for him, like any election anywhere, that is exactly how the system is supposed to work. If the majority of voters think candidates will do a good job protecting the value of their assets and enhancing the sense of community, they will be elected. If not, they won't. This is democracy in action.

Virtually all community associations are required to be transparent in their governance and operations. In fact, many states have laws requiring public board meetings and the availability of volumes of information to the members. Collectively, these "sunshine" laws ensure members access to regular meetings of the board and to the records of their associations.

As a result, board meetings in most states are open to the members, with the exception of legitimate executive sessions, and minutes generally are made available shortly after adjournment. Meeting notices and agendas typically are posted in advance, and members can arrange to address the board regarding issues of concern. Add to this the fact that most records of the association are open for inspection by members, and it becomes apparent that all the operations and finances of an association are available for scrutiny. Members thus are assured of the security of their funds and the responsible performance of their elected leaders.

Clearly, the key to effective community association governance is maintaining communication and interactions with homeowners while encouraging engagement, participation, and transparent operations.

DEPENDING ON VOLUNTEERS

Community associations are one of the purest forms of participatory democracy. They not only allow, but also encourage, participation of homeowners in every level of their operations and governance, essentially creating an atmosphere of common interest within the framework of the governing documents.

Many times the board will rely on committees for assistance. If so, the work of the association can be shared by more members. Committee volunteers usually simply want to contribute to the overall well-being of the association or want to be involved in the community in some fashion.

The board is responsible for creating committees, chartering them, appointing chairpersons and members, and acting on their recommendations for the benefit of the community. Typically the board appoints a committee chairperson and members who have expressed an interest or have expertise in the subject at hand.

With the exception of the architectural committee, which frequently is established in the CC&Rs, and the finance committee, which usually is required by the bylaws, most committees are created by the board. They have no intrinsic power and work at the will and direction of the board.

This system of a volunteer board and committee members seems to provide ample opportunity for members to participate in governance and to make positive contributions that help establish a community's sense of neighborhood identity that often is reflected in the value of resales.

SECURING PROFESSIONAL MANAGEMENT

Anyone who understands the challenges and complexities of community association management knows that community managers are a board's most valuable resource. As professional consultants and experts in their fields, community managers should play leadership roles in advising and assisting association boards of directors. Under no circumstances can they afford simply to respond to directives. Being passive or only reactive likely will result in missed opportunities, whether corrective or visionary in nature. Instead, community managers must be proactive in identifying ways to help the board excel.

To keep costs down, for example, association budgets have grown more detailed and complex. Enforcement procedures for rules and protective covenants have evolved into complicated processes designed to protect the rights of individuals and of the association. In many larger associations this has required volunteer board members to devote considerable time to keeping abreast of laws, regulations, and day-to-day operations of the community. Clearly, not many people have the time or expertise to run an association full time. As a result, many associations hire professional association management firms to help them fulfill their obligations.

Professional community association managers need to be knowledgeable and skilled in areas of budgeting, rules creation and enforcement, contract negotiation, vendor oversight, statutory parameters and updates affecting associations, high-level group and interpersonal communications, group dynamics, property management, customer service, election procedures, technology, and parliamentary procedures. They also must be familiar with contemporary professional standards regarding all aspects of association creation and operation. The list of essential areas of expertise is demanding. Used properly by the board, the manager is a wellspring of knowledge and information that can save the association time and money and add enormous value.

Without a professional manager, board members would need to master more than all of the skills listed and to find resources to keep abreast of legal updates and the newest best practices for operating communities successfully. Virtually no one elected to the board of a community association ever received training that would qualify him or her to operate a multimillion-dollar not-for-profit association. Most are simply well-meaning members who want to serve their communities. Many times the members are only marginally familiar with the candidates who run to serve on their board, and almost no state offers training to help them do their jobs efficiently and effectively.

Over time, the laws governing community associations in most states have grown more complex. Similarly, community association governing documents have tended to become more complicated and more specific in outlining the authorities and responsibilities of the association, the board, and the members.

According to most attorneys and experts in the field, a board can delegate all of its authority to a manager but none of its responsibility. While board members may delegate the day-to-day operations of the association to a management company, the board remains ultimately responsible to the members for the decisions it makes. It accomplishes this by providing oversight of the management company.

In short, the role of the professional community association manager and/or management company generally is to provide expertise in areas of property management, community governance, budgeting, and accounting services, as well as to offer advice and guidance that will assist the board in policy creation and implementation.

The management company typically is the liaison between the board and its members, vendors, professionals such as CPAs and attorneys, the public, and the government. The manager arranges meetings of the board and/or members, including securing a location, publishing notices of meetings, arranging elections, and securing and keeping all business records of the association. To assist the board in fulfilling its oversight role, the manager will submit written reports to the board about all pertinent activities and recommendations.

The board therefore monitors the association's progress toward its goals and its financial health, and it continually takes advantage of opportunities to improve the sense of community and the value of the assets.

As boards become more aware of their professional and personal limitations, they have begun employing more capable, sophisticated, and professional managers and using them as their best and most valuable resource. These highly trained and skilled professionals offer and deliver tremendous short- and long-term value.

Because of their experience and expertise, managers often help in unexpected ways. A manager of an association in the Southwest, for example, secured $4,000 in unpaid assessments and collection fees from the banker who wanted to sell a foreclosed condominium. The manager simply refused to provide the gate access code needed to secure access to the property until the delinquent account was paid in full. It was—within one week.

Board members were surprised and thrilled that one of their highest delinquencies had been paid. This may have been a small success, but the manager was proud to reflect her commitment to provide excellence in customer service. It is only one of countless examples of managers who proudly and gladly go above and beyond the call of duty for the associations they manage.

CONCLUSION

When critics write about and discuss community associations, they typically refer to incidents and association operational models from decades ago. Just as everything else in society matures and evolves, so have community associations. Today's associations are open, transparent, and welcoming places to live where every member can contribute in positive ways.

Organizations, including the national CAI through its local chapters' programs and national webinars, and the Executive Council of Homeowners in California provide targeted educational programs for association board members and homeowners. These programs are designed specifically to help participants understand their roles in operating their associations. Wise management companies also offer extensive continuing education and orientation programs for board members, homeowners, and community managers.

As a result of these and other efforts, many associations have adopted a more successful and professional model of operations than ever before. The main beneficiaries of these changes are the members and the professionals who serve them. Undoubtedly, the growth and success of community associations witnessed over the past forty years will continue as the industry evolves and the lifestyle is enjoyed by even greater numbers of people. Understanding how community associations work will facilitate that process.

DAVID AND SANDRA
cherish their basic rights as homeowners

Myth: Homeowners give up their basic rights when they choose to live in a community association.

Buster: Community association rules are intended to benefit all homeowners and to protect and enhance property values. When purchasing homes in community associations, buyers agree to comply with the governing documents, including the bylaws and rules that can be amended by homeowners.

Understanding the rules is essential, and their enforcement by a third party can promote living in peace and harmony while minimizing conflicts between neighbors. Living in a community association depends on the democratic process and in no way violates homeowners' constitutional rights. Homeowners live there by choice.

David and Sandra experienced the advantage of rules early: Condo hunting was great fun for the energetic couple. They fell in love with a new condominium with amenities galore: an outdoor patio overlooking the pool, lots of room for seating and a grill, a chef's kitchen with granite and stainless steel appliances, and a clubhouse perfect for entertaining. In their excitement to "just get the keys," however, they didn't read the condominium rules.

The two were very proud of their first home and thoroughly enjoyed the freedom that condo ownership afforded them. It was great to have someone else "taking care of it all." One night, after arriving home from a long business trip, Sandra noticed that several balconies overlooking the pool were draped with towels. This seemed understandable at first.

Week after week, though, the untidy appearance of those towels increasingly bothered Sandra, which was surprising, as she had always considered herself pretty flexible and tolerant. She found herself noticing more items that seemed out of place in the area, and she wasn't really sure what to do. How could she introduce herself to her neighbors by complaining about their behavior? That certainly could result in negative relationships and encourage continuing conflicts.

While talking to David about it, they recalled that the contract they signed at their closing had a list of the condominium association's rules. Reading them for the first time, she realized that they offered a good avenue toward resolving her problem. Soon after she emailed a request to her board of directors, her mission was accomplished: The towels disappeared from the patios, and the pool area was kept tidy for the rest of the summer.

Sandra and David were glad they had a third party like the condo's board to facilitate a reminder about the rules. Asking neighbors they didn't know yet to clean their patios surely would have made for awkward introductions. By enforcing these rules, the board promoted peace and harmony while protecting the property's appearance and value and also respecting members' rights under the rules. They did so without violating anybody's constitutional rights.

FREQUENTLY ASKED QUESTIONS:

Q1: How do I know what type of association I live in?

A1: When you purchased your home you received a packet with a set of governing documents, including Articles of Incorporation. This document should define the type of association in which you live. If it is unclear, check the Declaration of Covenants, Conditions, and Restrictions (CC&Rs), which also should be in your packet.

Q2: How can I review the records of the association?

A2: To review your community association's records, contact the secretary of the board of directors or the community association manager, if there is one. Ask for an appointment to go to the association's registered place of business to review the documents. You will save time and effort if you tell him or her ahead of time which records you want to examine. If you need copies of any records, be prepared to pay for the copy service.

You will not be allowed to examine records from executive sessions of the board of directors, as most state laws define those materials as privileged and confidential. If you have questions about this matter, please consult your attorney, as different states handle this information in different ways.

Q3: How do boards of directors foster community spirit?

A3: Boards of directors will adopt different priorities and strategies for promoting community spirit. Their choices typically reflect the needs and interests of the residents whom they represent. Many organize and host special activities such as holiday celebrations, yard beautification contests, guest speaker series, and pool parties.

Q4: What is the best way to get involved in my association?

A4: Associations are almost always looking for volunteers to serve on committees, help organize events, and run for election to the board of directors. Go to a board meeting or contact a board member or the association manager to discuss your areas of interest and the best opportunities to get involved. Chances are you'll be amazed at the variety of activities that will suit your interests and time availability.

Q5: How can I serve on a committee or ask the board to appoint a committee to address an issue that I consider important?

A5: Boards of directors rely on volunteers and should welcome opportunities to involve them. First, find out whether your board already appointed a committee that has responsibilities related to your interest. If so, ask to be appointed at the first opportunity, and volunteer to attend committee meetings and to participate in activities. If not, consider writing a letter to the board. Be sure to include suggestions for the committee's name, responsibilities, and opportunities to be of assistance in promoting community spirit.

CHAPTER 2

Why Many People Prefer Community Associations

For a community to be whole and healthy, it must be
based on people's love and concern for each other.

—MILLARD FULLER
Founder of Habitat for Humanity

INTRODUCTION

The emotional equity that results in a sense of community depends
on balancing individual needs and priorities with those of others.
Such a commitment to mutual benefits and to common interests is
one of the keys to successful community association living. Consistent with Millard Fuller's words, the healthiest and most wholesome
neighborhoods typically are defined by good neighbors who develop
genuine affection and concern for each other.

Community associations depend on a democratic decision-making process to serve their members while protecting their property
values. Homeowners who appreciate this sense of mutual support
typically are among the many people who prefer to live in community
associations. They can realize their American dream by choosing to
live in a community association and serve their economic self-interest
while enjoying a better quality of life. Those elements of their decision-making processes are discussed in this chapter.

REALIZING THE AMERICAN DREAM

Exactly why do so many homeowners choose to live in a community association? Simply phrased, they want to realize the American dream in the easiest, most cost-effective way that satisfies their needs immediately while safeguarding their future. Community associations place ideal circumstances within their reach.

Imagine, for example, a community association with nicely manicured grounds and flowers in bloom every start of spring. Nearby amenities like swimming pools and clubhouses are accessible, suitable, and appealing. Roads are well maintained, and street signage is sharp and freshly painted. There are never too many cars parked in front of houses (unless it's Super Bowl weekend), and patrol cars drive through periodically to reduce safety concerns.

A community manager regularly inspects the association to spot any deeply troubling or flagrant rules violations or maintenance conditions requiring attention. These include trash bins not fastened, an open invitation to undesirable four-legged creatures; visible water damage to wood trim or dry rot, a costly expense to repair later if not treated properly now; or trash cans or building materials left in the open for a prolonged period, making the neighborhood look cluttered or at least less than perfectly desirable.

A new member of an association, for example, experienced an uncomfortable "Big Brother is watching" feeling when a manager called to ask her to remove her trash bin from the curb. The homeowner complained that the offending container had been there only one hour past the deadline and that the enforcer was being overly picky.

After discussing it with a relative who was experienced in association living, however, she understood the necessity for enforcing the rules timely and uniformly. She realized that the manager was looking out for the best interests of the community by ensuring that unsightly bins were removed promptly. Based on this shared insight, the homeowner understood and supported the rule.

When major or minor infractions like these occur, the community manager's goal is to correct them immediately, swiftly, and effectively, before they become more serious and require the board's attention. By also explaining why the violated rules exist and how their enforcement benefits offenders, managers are more likely to promote understanding and compliance. Above all, they should enforce rules uniformly, reasonably, and fairly.

These ideal circumstances are an added inducement for homeowners to choose community associations—in addition to the wisdom of protecting and enhancing their property values.

As proudly diverse as North America is, there is no single, unifying, Norman Rockwell–style American dream for home and community, except perhaps the following:

> We want to live in an environment in which we feel safe.

> We want a home we can call "our own."

> We want to believe that over the long term the property value of our home will be at least maintained and at best appreciate, thus increasing our overall financial health for ourselves and, if applicable, our family.

This realistic and attainable American dream for home and community is realized daily by millions of property owners—regardless of property type. Needs and expectations are different for those in community associations composed of single-family homes versus high-rise condominiums, mixed-use communities (which blend residential and commercial occupancy), active adult (catering to the fifty-five-year-old plus crowd), or other residential properties. Despite their differences, these property types mostly share the three criteria defined above because they satisfy our overall need to be economically, societally, and individually fulfilled. Homeownership is part of the realistic and attainable American dream—the ability for a wider range of citizens to reach that dream and experience the slice of lifestyle idealized and realized for any and all economic and demographic groups.

CHOOSING TO LIVE IN
COMMUNITY ASSOCIATIONS

A longstanding argument against community associations is the false allegation that potential homeowners have no choice but to concede and live in—and be governed by—an association. This argument has several logical flaws. It is true that over the past forty years community associations have seen an amazing increase in the number of properties they govern. It bears repeating that their estimated growth was from 701,000 housing units in 10,000 communities governed by associations in 1970 to 25.1 million units in 314,200 communities in 2011.

On a related note, the 1970 U.S. Census reported 68,684,000 housing units within its boundaries. Given the Community Association Institute's estimate of housing units governed, that means only 1.02 percent of the country's housing units at that time were in community associations—a minuscule percentage. Forty years later, by comparison, the 2010 Census reported that the number of housing units nearly doubled to 137,368,000. What a boom. Given CAI estimates, 18.05 percent of those units were governed by a community association. This was a significant increase but indicated that less than 20 percent of housing units are in community associations. Because more than 80 percent of households in the United States are not in community associations, clearly, home buyers have a choice. It is simultaneously true, however, that where population density is an issue, new construction is likely to be in an association, thereby limiting choices in that area.

Analyzed over forty years, the percentage gain of housing units in community associations from 1.02 to 20 has not been terribly dramatic, but it is a steady percentage gain nonetheless. While community associations have increased in size and percentage, those same homes are in the overwhelming minority of housing units by more than four to one. To say that home buyers do not have a choice is intellectually dishonest.

Demand for community associations

Business shifts impact the demand for community associations. As these demands vary, three major factors typically interact in defining and in meeting the need and purpose of specific types of communities: developers/builders, municipalities needing tax revenue, and lifestyle preferences.

In the 1960s and 1970s, when one thought of a general semblance of community associations, it was usually in the form of either an urban, or downtown, high-rise or multiunit building (such as the traditional co-op or condominium) or of a gated, ultra-luxury community. Both kinds of properties were limited to select audiences: city dwellers and the megarich. Both audiences had finite markets, and while this market remained stagnant throughout the 1970s, the global economic boom of the 1980s took hold. As two-income households exploded over single-wage household earners, significantly more home buyers had more disposable income with which to attain lifestyle desires.

This upwardly mobile trend translated to greater demand for attaining more leisure time, more and better amenities, and what many might consider an overall richer lifestyle. It didn't hurt that, in addition to more disposable income, the consumerism of the 1980s was fueled by pop culture and over-the-top aspirational television series such as *Dallas* and *Dynasty*.

As consumers increased demand, housing developers and builders filled the gap. They capitalized on building less exclusive and less urban communities, primarily in suburban areas of larger metropolitan areas, and then on scaling additional middle-tier metropolitan areas. While some described the consequence as a flight to suburbia, the reality is much more pragmatic: Land was cheaper in the suburbs than in the city and thus easier and more profitable to attain and develop. As a result, community association development exploded. The CAI table in Chapter 1 indicates its housing units more than quadrupled from 1970 to 3.6 million housing units in approximately

36,000 communities in the 1980s and further expanded to 11.6 million housing units in 130,000 communities by 1990.

The correlation between the growth patterns of housing units and community associations is natural, if not immediately obvious: Developers embraced community associations to maintain continuity and control in building projects as the number of housing units per building project increased over time. This allowed them to exploit economies of scale and to maximize revenue for pent-up consumer demand. Such continuity and control provided stability in housing values and marketability of developers' various building projects. While some housing and community projects justifiably earned the "cookie cutter" description, they were a very safe buy for new buyers.

Market growth continued in 2000: 17.8 million housing units in 222,500 communities were governed by an association. As the market grew, it did so—and through growth cycles, it continues to do so—because of consumer demand.

This is pure consumer demand in play: Homeowners choose to live in community associations despite many other attractive choices available in the market. Community associations have grown beyond the single one-size-fits-all or cookie-cutter approach, instead mirroring the growing diversity of the North American workforce and culture.

Responding to diverse demands, today's community associations fit every possible lifestyle and economic range. Developers help create increasingly customized community associations to satisfy the demand, and they tailor communities by grounds plan and location to attract specific groups such as active adults older than fifty-five, young adults without children, and adults with young children. Often they provide audience-specific amenities; more planned activities; fewer common areas, but mixing a residential with a hip commercial district; or more playgrounds and longer, wider walking trails to accommodate strollers.

These kinds of benefits attract individuals and families of all ages, races/ethnicities, lifestyles, economics, and backgrounds. Their common interests enhance the likelihood of their becoming good neighbors.

Range of community associations

Because diverse demands impact the available range of community associations, they are not limited to a property type or socioeconomic level. They include cooperatives, condominiums, and single-family homes; and homeowners can choose their preferred level by choosing their preferred type of community association. Likewise, part of the appeal of community associations is their range of community types, which is broader than those typically portrayed by critics or by those who like to stereotype.

The easy (and lazy) picture to paint of community associations is one of single-family houses, all in a row, even roof pitches, and all painted within a hair of a tint of each other. This is the stereotype epitomized in Malvina Reynolds's 1962 hit song, "Little Boxes." While communities of this type still exist (and have their appeal to certain homeowners), the truth is far more diverse.

There also is a persistent misunderstanding that community associations have the power or intent to discriminate against federally protected classes by refusing to allow purchases by these minority groups. Make no mistake: Discrimination sadly still exists in this world, but to assume that community associations cause the discrimination is shortsighted and erroneous.

Community associations are composed of members who join the association through a property purchase. Members are neither elected nor approved by some secret committee. They join when they buy a piece of property within an association.

The exceptions are Cooperative Housing Associations. Persons who buy into cooperatives do so by purchasing shares that entitle them to live in their units by virtue of what is called a "proprietary lease." This lease is granted by the cooperative board that represents the shareholders of the cooperative and has the right to establish certain nondiscriminatory criteria for allowing the purchase of shares by potential buyers.

Today's homeowners can choose their community associations in nearly any configuration they wish: single-family homes, condominiums, commercial/residential mixes (otherwise known as mixed use), cooperatives, resort, and more. Why the range of diversity? Market demand.

Those who live and wish to live in a community association represent a wide and varied mix, reflecting a myriad of personal backgrounds, incomes, and demographics. The market segment appeal of community associations is based more on age and family status (single, married, married without children, married with children, empty nesters, etc.) and not on the common critical cry of class- and race-based discrimination.

Today's growing appeal of the wide range of community associations is exactly the opposite of being exclusionary in that they are more accessible to all. Even the most exclusive in terms of meeting expensive standards of excellence do not exclude racial, ethnic, religious, or other minorities. Given the diversity of community associations, economic and social factors are important, but in ways that attract all kinds of potential homeowners.

SERVING ECONOMIC SELF-INTEREST

At the heart of property ownership is economic self-interest. Homeowners normally expect a positive return on their investment. Their homes usually are the biggest economic piece of their financial portfolios. During the long term, they expect property values to appreciate, despite short-term setbacks that devaluate them or artificial bubbles that inflate value beyond realistic margins.

Protection of property values

One of the main goals of community associations is simply one of economic value: to protect and enhance the value of the property. This may lead to rules such as no exposed trash bins or unapproved lawn decorations or plantings, regular upkeep of external physical property, etc. While such restrictions may be controversial for some, the vast majority of community associations maintain a pragmatic approach to protecting property values.

Consider the alternative perspective: Why does the value of a property decrease? In creating a community association, a developer spends potentially millions of dollars advertising it to the greater market. This often includes professionally designed brochures; open houses for real estate agents; billboards; and newspaper, radio, and television advertising. The purpose is to create value by creating awareness of the property. A builder who is finished selling the property also is finished advertising the joy of living in the association. The community association is left on its own to compete against all other existing and new properties that are being heavily advertised by another (or even by the same) builder.

Property values presumably will be affected as the market's memory fades and natural competition for prospective buyers accelerates. They certainly will decrease if the property experiences little upkeep, uncertainty of long-term ability to maintain the property, and ambiguity regarding whether the surrounding area will maintain its long-term viability and sustainability. In other words, if people don't know what's going on to maintain or improve the property, it's highly unlikely that its value will increase appreciably.

Community associations can help maintain a sense of control of a property to enhance its value. They help make investments in property "safer" by establishing and projecting sound management, expectations, and predictability. This can be facilitated partly by interacting continuously with real estate agents, including providing them with simple, ongoing marketing materials; offering them continuing education and outreach programs; and even participating in their local real estate trade associations.

An association property, while susceptible to market conditions and to other changes in external factors, is controlled more tightly than a nonassociation property, thus reducing some of the unpredictable variables that cause greater value fluctuations. Information is more readily and easily available about what is being purchased in an association than about nonassociation property. By taking away much of the uncertainty about the property and providing simple, ongoing marketing pieces, community associations generally do a better job of providing owners with a higher degree of protected property values.

Reinvestment in neighborhoods

Community associations can improve the appearance of neighborhoods in ways that local governments typically cannot. Their reinvestment is of significant value, particularly because it is unique to association-governed properties.

The importance of the curb appeal of homes in a property, including single-family homes and multiunit dwellings, cannot be underestimated. It immediately conjures up how the main property looks: Does it have a nice structure? Does the current owner maintain internal elements at the same level as external facades? Are there any foundation issues? Other factors are at play here, including the other properties in the neighborhood and the community's infrastructure, including roads, landscaping, and signage.

Local and state governments are challenged more than ever to balance their budgets while operating under increasing costs and limited abilities to raise income to meet shortfalls. The State of Texas, for example, slashed its budget for 2012–13 to make-up for a $27 billion deficit. The State of California's income in 2012 was expected to fall short of anticipated costs by $10 billion or more. Significant reductions in state funding inevitably have repercussions at the local levels. When governments have no choice but to cut all but the most essential costs, they invariably look for ways to defray the costs and related responsibilities.

Community associations offer a private enterprise solution to part of these budget conundrums: They often maintain their own infrastructures, including water, sewer, roads, streets, street signs, landscaping, and even security. Beyond those basic but important needs, they often also enhance the neighborhood's appearance by enforcing standards and by offering attractive amenities such as parks, pools, and clubhouses. No one could blame local government officials for welcoming this "assistance."

Critics of community associations, however, often cast this positive aspect in a negative light. They harp on the concept of double taxation, arguing that associations create a "double-taxing" situation because homeowners have to pay not only local and state taxes but also community assessments. This seemingly logical argument is rebutted easily, however, by the obvious differences: Community associations provide a higher degree of economic control over appropriating assessments; can respond more timely and effectively; and almost universally surpass local government's standards for maintaining roads, streets, signs, and landscaping. Under no circumstances are homeowners paying twice for the same items that would be available at the same time. Community association residents are paying for a higher standard and a better, faster response.

While the criticism of double taxation initially seems to be based on a logical assumption, common sense and history dictate a different reality: Local governments do not always look out for an individual's or neighborhood's best interests and cannot always respond timely.

Operating with a set revenue base that is limited by taxes and bonds, a city, town, or other municipal body must improve numerous properties, including many that are not residential. Consequently, it spreads these property improvement investments over the needs of the many, not the needs of one or of some.

Community associations, by comparison, keep their investments in the community proper. The reality is that what is assessed by a community association is allocated to that same community association. It's a more direct form of investment and reinvestment in the same community.

ENJOYING A BETTER QUALITY OF LIFE

A few property owners may have unlimited or nearly unlimited access to capital to build streets and other necessary infrastructure for a functional home and desired quality of life. The reality is, however, that most property owners do not. In democratizing homeownership in a community association, owners have collective abilities to improve their homes, neighborhoods, and communities through the power of all owners contributing to the costs of all construction, maintenance needs, and amenities of a community.

Community associations offer the benefits of a better quality of life associated with a critical mass of monies that can be dedicated to maintaining the necessary infrastructure needs of members, enhanced by bargaining power to decrease potential costs. While it would be nearly impossible for individuals to pay for these expenses, collectively, homeowners in the association can bear the same costs. The economic advantages of community associations are therefore far-reaching, buoyed by a diverse range of social and cultural activities in desirable housing.

Social activities

Although community associations clearly offer the economic benefits related to value protection and cost-efficiency scales, they also offer softer social benefits that vary according to their members' needs and interests. Clearly, many homeowners choose to live in community associations because they value the emotional equity that families earn by living in a neighborhood that brings people together.

Community associations recreate the traditional bonds on which communities and neighborhoods were built. While many may be nostalgic for the days of tighter, more neighborly bonds, the reality is that today's professional and societal norms are different. The workday is longer, commuters may drive farther, technology and the media impact demands for activities, and home businesses facilitate 24/7 commitments.

Simultaneously, families with more than one adult who works full time may have less leisure time. Those with children under eighteen may want more organized activities such as league sports, volunteer opportunities, and part-time work. Even seniors in active adult communities may want more activity options than ever.

Opportunities for enjoying pure leisure time with neighbors are condensed, if not rare, for many families. Without community associations and organized activities, they are challenged to connect and to develop meaningful, positive, non-work-related relationships.

Enter community associations: Instead of being the exclusionary entities sometimes described by critics, they have evolved into a melting pot of interests and activities. These include National Night Out (a national observance of neighborhood and community), safety awareness events, restaurant tastings, and national holiday observances through community parties, family events, and more. Only the imagination and willingness of association members limit their opportunities to connect with neighbors who share their interests.

A community association in the West Coast offers an example of the unifying and strengthening impact of social activities. Founded after World War II and comprising two hundred mass-produced inexpensive homes, the community's amenities were limited to a modest but functional clubhouse and a very nice pool at a central park. Apathy was rampant, evidenced by lack of participation and general disinterest in the operation and well-being of the association. Problems focused on half-open garage doors and nonassociation neighbors sneaking into the pool.

According to community lore, at some point someone suggested organizing a Fourth of July parade. It was an immediate success, especially for children and their parents. The tradition persists, and today the newest member of the community is invited to be the official grand marshal. The parade ends at the clubhouse in the park with a "bring your own meat" community BBQ.

Inspired by this huge hit, volunteers organized other events that were equally enjoyable. The Annual Membership Meeting evolved into a fun-filled celebration: Post-business meeting festivities included a band, lots of food donated by members and local grocers, and even a college scholarship funded by voluntary contributions.

Relationships improved not only within the association but also beyond its boundaries. The Annual Meeting Party attracted so much attention that tickets were sold to nonassociation members and generally were sold out early. Problems with the unauthorized use of the pool were resolved as the association voted to sell memberships to residents of the surrounding community instead of fighting the losing battle of keeping them out.

The happy result? The association funds part of its budget and most of its reserve with these revenues from nonmembers. Simultaneously, it has improved the quality of life of homeowners and raised its profile with local real estate agents. This is a real public relations coup!

Perhaps the most interesting aspect of this real-life example is that the stick-frame production homes were built in what is now one of the most expensive neighborhoods of the Bay Area peninsula. The homes have more than retained their value, partly because of their location but largely because of the rousing community spirit that the association promoted among its members and the larger municipality in which it is located.

This is a wonderful example of how social activities can be opportunities to build community bonds by connecting with neighbors and other community members. They typically bring together individuals or families who share social likenesses such as having children in the same school and enjoying similar interests. Community associations accentuate these community bonds as they develop their unique cultures.

Cultural diversity

A community will build its own culture while building its own emotional equity with its individual members. That culture can vary as much as the increasingly diverse range of backgrounds, race/ethnicity, ages, religions, interests, and occupations within today's community associations. Those very differences among association members can be a great source of conversation and learning.

The same heterogeneity is evident for other demographic groups. It simply is not true that community associations are homogeneous havens for white residents in similar higher-than-average income categories behind isolating gates and walls. Given the demographics reported earlier, this might have been a valid case in the 1970s and 1980s, but in the 1990s and beyond, it is a shortsighted, uninformed, and incorrect argument. Access to community associations is only a matter of economics, location, and lifestyle choice for most members, and these issues impact buyers across all racial/ethnic, professional, social, and economic strata.

Community associations do not set the patterns of living; they follow them. The United States and North America are increasingly diverse, reflecting the greater diversity among homeowners in all urban, suburban, and rural living environments. Their pattern of living reflects the changing racial/ethnic and economic demographic diversity.

Any discussion about community associations inevitably reverts to the pattern of living for ethnic and economic demographic spectrum of diversity. This is important because it is what continues to drive the business and personal living phenomenon of community association living. The facts underscore that community associations reflect the changing housing patterns throughout the country and take the lead from market demands.

Housing pattern diversity

Housing demands skyrocketed among all socioeconomic groups in the 2000s, given the ease of borrowing money at that time. While this was a bubble-like market condition, it created a group of new homeowners who desired and demanded a sense of community and neighborhoods to call their own. Developers and builders could hardly keep up with the demand, whether real or artificially inflated, for entry-level homes. These new communities were spurred by market demand and reflected ethnically and financially diverse homeowners.

The boom gave birth to the inevitable question: Can community associations influence housing patterns? Yes, but they are not, as some critics claimed, an unstoppable, kudzu-like force of nature that determines them. Instead, they reflect market-driven housing patterns and adapt their offerings because of changing demands. While community associations are more of the built-in amenity variety, the majority of newly built communities are a condition of the market demand to protect economic and social investments. The variety and level of amenities will differ in community associations, mostly because of economics.

Community associations affect housing patterns positively. Some will attest that their favorable impact on housing patterns has been pronounced in virtually every metropolitan area by attracting suburbanites back to urban areas or by creating neighborhoods and communities in blighted suburban and/or inner city areas. As a result, community associations open the entry-level housing market to millions of individuals and families that otherwise could not afford to own their own homes.

A related result is that urban living now is considered stylish, especially by young professionals interested in refurbished or newly constructed urban or downtown communities. There is a strong demand from those interested in moving back to downtown areas in community associations with tailored amenities that make city living more convenient and time saving.

Worksite changes

The globalization of our world in general also impacts the economic diversity reflected by community associations. Adapting to worksite changes, for example, many associations changed or reinterpreted their rules to allow home businesses that meet certain criteria. This reflects their knowledge that technology enables professionals to work remotely, making geographic boundaries less important. Concurrently, steady high-speed Internet connections enable businesses to look more for top talent (wherever that talent may be) rather than requiring physical workplace attendance in a traditional office setting. As a result, talented professionals can roam or stay exactly where they are. Their key demands may no longer be related to where they will have to live or move for a job, but where they can find a suitable home in which to work, play, and live.

With these changing needs in these changing times, community associations are not exclusionary but can be exclusive. They reflect the neighborhood and are just another amenity. Whether home buyers are looking for a starter single-family home in a gated community that includes a school and a place of worship or a high-end, high-rise luxury condominium with a 360-degree view, they can find the perfect match. Community associations are a unifying means for bringing together homeowners with similar desires and needs. They are not the neighborhood; they simply reflect the neighborhood and represent a safe amenity to living.

CONCLUSION

Homeownership in community associations boils down primarily to two main factors: economic and social best interests. Homeowners want their property to appreciate in value while they feel safe and make emotional connections to their homes and their communities.

Community associations make the connection between the head and the heart by instituting necessary steps to protect property values and providing means through which to connect to the community through amenities, events, volunteerism, and other functions. While community associations are no guarantee for value appreciation and a tangible sense of community, they do provide the blueprint and process more so than any other nonassociation option. This is why community associations have grown in number, respect, and demand while meeting the needs of homeowners reflecting increasingly diverse socioeconomic groups, races/ethnicities, and ages over the past forty years.

DAVID AND SANDRA
prefer the community association lifestyle

Myth: Because community association developments have become pervasive, homeowners have no choice about living in them.

Buster: Every homeowner has a choice of home and can decide whether to live in a community governed by a community association. Buying decisions usually are impacted by price, location, lifestyle, special amenities, commute options, maintenance standards, and a medley of advantages/disadvantages. Never is any buyer forced to live in an association; it is a choice.

David and Sandra chose their second home in a community association, partly because of the rich variety of amenities and organized activities, the impressive maintenance standards, and their freed time. After owning their condominium for five years, they were ready to grow their family beyond their two adopted cats. Having sold their condo quickly, they were on a serious hunt for a single-family home. The couple, soon to be parents, had so much more to consider: Which is the best school district? Is a park within walking distance? Can they afford a pool, or should they find a community with a pool? How big a yard can they or do they want to handle? What amenities and activities are available nearby? How much time and effort will be required for maintenance? Is the home in a safe area? Do homes hold their values better in one neighborhood than another? Getting their priorities straight was their first hurdle. Once focused, they began a search that would prove beneficial.

David and Sandra's three-bedroom, two-bathroom starter home gave them years of enjoyment and an emotional equity they had not expected. Soon they were a family of four who grew together in their home while transforming neighbors into friends. Sandra quit her job after their second child was born, and, with a tighter budget, found many ways to have fun using the community's amenities and exploring the local world with their children.

An easy walk to the community park meant outdoor exercise and lots of fun for the kids who treasured "their" playground. Meeting other families there became a mainstay in their lives, which led Sandra to making her first "Mom" friends. Play dates at each other's homes led to the mothers organizing a social committee, and, before Sandra knew it, she was working with the association's board to budget and plan seasonal community events.

The most attended and beloved event was the Annual Fourth of July Bike and Trike Parade. Every family, every child, and even some dogs, cycled and walked through the neighborhood with red, white, and blue streamers flying behind them. The parade ended at the community pool for a swim party, and David led the volunteers in the hot dog grilling that lasted throughout the day.

Such great friends and memories were made while living in this community. Sandra and David knew they had made the right choice: They chose to live in a community association that offered many enriching activities for their young family. No one forced them to make this choice. It was a conscious decision they made together that perfectly fit their personalities and family lifestyle with benefits that could be found only in a community association.

FREQUENTLY ASKED QUESTIONS

Q1: Does living in a community association guarantee the value of my home will be protected?

A1: There are no guarantees regarding home values, but protecting and enhancing property values are the top priority of community associations. Their focus is not merely on individual homes but, rather, on the entire property, including its infrastructure and amenities. Accordingly, homes within them are more likely to retain and improve their values than homes in nonassociation communities. This assertion is supported by a study by the American Enterprise Institute that indicates that homes within a community association have a minimum 5–6 percent price premium.

Homeowners who do not live in an association-governed community can work independently or with neighbors to protect and improve their property values. Those who do can depend on their respective associations.

Q2: If I am supplementing the municipal tax system, are my assessments tax deductible?

A2: No, assessments are not tax deductible. Neither are you supplementing the municipal tax system, however. Home buyers choose to live in a community association—or not. Those who do, reap the benefits of an improved civil infrastructure typically provided in these communities. Assessments are appropriated to meet a higher standard of living and to offer a better quality of life than otherwise would be provided by local governments.

Q3: Why are buyers forced to live in a community association when looking to move to a more suburban environment?

A3: Home buyers are not forced to live in a community association, even when looking for a home in a suburban environment. There are many rural, suburban, and metropolitan neighborhoods without community associations. Only approximately 20 percent of the housing units in the United States are in community associations, proving that home buyers have many alternatives. Living in an association is a personal choice and should be examined as such. The value of either choice truly is an individual decision.

Q4: I would rather live in a house than in a condominium but travel regularly and don't have the time or want the responsibility of maintenance. What kind of community association is best for me?

A4: Your best choice may be a single-family home that is part of a Planned Unit Development. In addition to offering the housing choice you are looking for, PUDs, as they often are called, generally offer amenities such as pools, parks, clubhouses, and even golf courses. Front yard maintenance often is the responsibility of the association, while many residents hire landscape maintenance companies to care for their respective side and back yards. The real key is always to check with the association or its management company before buying to ascertain your maintenance responsibility.

Q5: If I buy a condominium in a multiunit building, how can I be certain I will get along with my neighbors? Should the prospect of living in close proximity to so many people be a concern?

A5: When buying a condominium unit, consider this important point: There may be neighbors living above, below, and beside you. To ensure your future peace of mind, make certain that proper soundproofing was installed when the unit was constructed. Also check the association rules and CC&Rs to determine whether they are acceptable to you and fit your lifestyle. Finally, understand that the condominium is a community. As in all communities and neighborhoods, it is the responsibility of everyone to practice good citizenship and neighborliness. Most condominium communities attract neighbors who are considerate, conscientious, and enjoy the camaraderie and convenience of association living. If problems do arise, they often are resolved easily by the board. The reason is obvious: Most condominium residents realize that one of the keys to enjoying the lifestyle is reasonableness if and when disputes arise.

Q6: What guarantees that there is no discrimination in the community association model?

A6: Community associations have no governing or legal authority to make a community exclusive based on factors such as race, ethnicity, national origin, gender, or religion. Their main purpose is to serve the community by protecting property values and increasing emotional equity in the community.

CHAPTER 3

Why Community Associations Will Continue to Thrive

An association of men who will not quarrel with one another
is a thing which has never yet existed, from the greatest
confederacy of nations down to a town meeting or a vestry.

—THOMAS JEFFERSON

INTRODUCTION

The continuously increasing demand for living in community associations is steeped in consumers' interest in enjoying a better quality
of life and access to appropriately appealing amenities. It also reflects
their desire to enhance their property values while reducing their
time-consuming outdoor maintenance chores. While Thomas Jefferson was right that members of associations will quarrel, the most successful organizations afford means for debate, discussion, consensus
building, and problem solving. The results of such exchanges are more
likely to reap satisfaction and positive attitudes.

This is particularly true of community associations. They offer ave-
nues through which members can resolve their differences while pri-
oritizing their mutual needs and interests, all through the democratic
process. Equally important, their growth reflects the strengthening
of their services and raising their standards based partly on lessons
learned through experience, successes, and controversies.

Why will community associations continue to thrive? The answer is simple: Given the data, it is easy to project their continued success. Their outlook reflects their ability to adapt to changing expectations and demographics, coupled with unchanging interests in protecting property values while enjoying a better quality of life.

This is not self-serving rhetoric espoused by promoters. It is substantiated by a series of surveys attesting that community associations are a desired lifestyle and that the overwhelming majority of homeowners are satisfied. A 2009 Zogby International poll of homeowners living in community associations, for example, indicated that a resounding 71 percent expressed a positive overall experience living in a community association, while only 12 percent expressed a negative opinion. Zogby's 2005 and 2007 polls showed remarkably similar results. All three were commissioned by the Research Foundation of the CAI. This impressive degree of satisfaction gives credence to the expectation that community association living is thriving and will continue to be in demand. The rationale for that expectation is examined in this chapter.

EXPANDING DEMAND FOR COMMUNITY ASSOCIATIONS

The projected continued and expanding demand for community associations is based on their sound history of changing with the times. Community association living in the United States didn't emerge overnight. It evolved by responding to needs, expectations, and, yes, even criticism.

The early years of suburban migration saw housing developments established in expanding municipalities that were adjacent to urban cities. These suburban towns generally offered homes with yards for children to play in, neighborhoods populated with similar families, and municipal services and facilities that could be supported by this new tax base. The access to municipal parks and recreational facilities offered an attractive option to the perceived limitations and inescapable concrete of urban living. It was a great place to raise a family, with neighborhoods in which each family maintained its own home and lot and complied with the local ordinances, while ideally making honest efforts to be good neighbors. Generally, the suburbs offered small town familiarity with nearby big-city amenities.

This post–World War II rise in American suburban living marked the start of the baby boom. When available land in these "bedroom" communities became scarce or expensive, development sprawled outward, and growing families followed. Suburban living became highly desirable.

Then came events that contributed greatly to creating and expanding demand for community associations. By the end of the 1960s and into the early '70s, inflation and unemployment were at historically high rates. The previously accepted theories of economic cycles of inflation and unemployment working in opposition suddenly propelled both to previously unimagined high levels. Coupled with the rising cost of oil, this created an atmosphere of rising costs, high interest rates, and lowered housing demand.

Municipalities began to see their property tax revenue, which had already suffered due to the previously discussed flight to the suburbs, shrink even more, creating atmospheres of fiscal crisis in small and large cities alike. Clearly, something had to change. The old models of fiscal and municipal planning no longer worked.

Land developers began to stimulate housing demand by reducing the cost of new housing. They did this by decreasing the cost of land through increasing density, converting inner-city apartment buildings into condominiums and cooperatives and thereby inventing community associations as a means of meeting this altered demand for housing. Their actions were viewed as a highly needed lifeline by the towns, cities, and municipalities. Officials understood the benefits of their tax base being expanded by higher density housing, with someone else paying for the infrastructure improvements and maintenance.

In retrospect, the concept of community associations grew out of demand created by a series of economic events that rendered the prior housing model economically obsolete. Community associations became a game changer by meeting the needs of buyers, developers, and municipalities. The question remained: Would more affordable housing satisfy the lifestyle and cultural needs of the modern public?

EVOLVING TO MEET CHANGING NEEDS

The concept of community associations evolved phenomenally for a variety of reasons. From meager beginnings, today's 314,200 community associations that house 62.3 million residents developed by evolving while meeting changing needs. They may have been created somewhat by circumstance, but their growth and sustainability were no accident. Because of their success, community associations exist throughout the country and are becoming prevalent in many parts of the world.

"Associations" initially were formed to provide affordable housing and to offset the dwindling availability of buildable land. Their developers and members soon realized, however, the associations' equally impressive ability to bring people with similar interests together in neighborhoods, to maintain and enhance the value of homes and of their community, to provide shared amenities, and to accommodate the changing work and lifestyle demands of a modern society. Although modified over time, those purposes persist. By continually evolving while meeting those changing needs, community associations will continue to prosper.

Affordable housing on dwindling land

The flight to the suburbs was based largely on the availability of cheap land. Over the course of time and because of the population explosion, however, land became scarcer and more expensive. Community associations that increased density allowed new housing starts to remain competitive with housing resales.

At the same time, cities began to experience decreased revenues caused by the "urban blight" of people moving to the suburbs' more affordable housing. They also experienced a new awakening as developers cost-effectively bought inner city apartment buildings and converted them into affordable condominiums. Their conversions began to stabilize inner city economies as they drew young professionals back from the suburbs. Eventually, however, this new housing was so successful that many cities passed ordinances to curtail their creation and sought to save available apartments for people who needed to rent rather than buy.

With a population of 311 million people in mid-2011, the United States is expected to grow to 400 million people in 2043, according to the 2010 U.S. Census. This means that the availability of buildable land will become even scarcer. Rest assured that community associations will come to the rescue, developing the appropriate affordable housing for its many different market segments.

Similar interests

Another strength of community associations is their ability to bring together people with similar interests. Families typically want to live in neighborhoods with others who share their needs, desires, and values. Those with young children, for example, may want to live in family-friendly neighborhoods with a rich variety of suitable activities, while many senior citizens would prefer dramatically different adult-friendly alternatives.

Facilities and services targeted for families interested in similar lifestyles help bring people together in desirable neighborhoods. A person concerned about safety may desire to live in a gated community, while one who enjoys swimming, fishing, or boating would look for a lake community. The design and nature of the community association can create the demand for its inherent product.

This is exactly where community associations excel and will continue to do so. Their developers analyze the markets, design appropriately appealing communities, collaborate with municipalities to fashion mutually beneficial arrangements, work with the necessary professionals to ensure a strong project, and attract home buyers. Finally, they devote themselves to a positive transition at the point that the community association assumes responsibility for a community. Strong beginnings will be the foundation from which community associations will continue to satisfy homeowners.

Property values

A first-time homebuyer may be most interested in getting a great value but soon will realize that the wisest course is to enhance the home's worth. Over time most homeowners learn that a property's value is affected not only by its maintenance and improvement but also by the surrounding properties and the community as a whole.

It would be almost impossible for an independent homeowner living outside a community association to control external factors such as the conditions of roads or the availability of amenities. This is where community associations are at their best: They protect the property value of homes in particular and of the community in general. Because these circumstances are unlikely to change, community associations are likely to be equally, if not more, appealing to homeowners in the future.

Shared amenities

Land developers realized long ago that the benefits of using shared amenities such as pools, parks, and clubhouses decreased with their distance from neighborhoods served and were considered advantages in purchasing decisions only if they were nearby. They solved this problem by providing amenities that were privatized for a community association. In doing so, they created demand for those amenities.

Even today, real estate advertising for individual homes routinely highlights the community amenities that are available to the purchaser. Because using amenities usually depends on their accessibility and convenience, making them part of the community association increases their use. Coupled with the ability of community association members to determine the level of availability, maintenance, and service of amenities, these are powerful tools for attracting buyers and satisfying residents. As homeowners become increasingly demanding and the population grows increasingly older and diverse, community associations are expected to rise to the challenge of providing amenity packages that will appeal to their targeted home buyers.

Work-life balance

Time is a precious commodity. Another benefit of a community association is saving homeowners the time they otherwise would have to spend maintaining their amenities and/or properties. Depending on the structure of their community associations, homeowners may perform some, very little, or even none of their home maintenance. This lack of maintenance responsibility remains a major attraction for most people who choose to live in a community association. It frees their time to spend on other activities by relieving them of most routine maintenance chores, including maintaining their lawns, landscaping, and all common areas and amenities. Doing so allows homeowners more time to use the amenities. An added value is that the regular maintenance typically enhances property values.

As career demands and work-related time commitments have increased over the decades, having less responsibility for home care is an attractive way to improve the work-life balance. This advantage will continue to make community association living particularly attractive to families with two wage earners, especially if they have children, and to homeowners who have little interest in performing maintenance chores.

DEVELOPING EMOTIONAL EQUITY

Successful community associations also have a strong sense of community that fosters participation and volunteerism. Their very nature requires volunteers because elected board members serve without compensation and often need committees to help manage communities. The importance and responsibility of these volunteers is underscored by a realization of the community's worth: Even a small three hundred-unit association with average home values of $250,000 represents $75 million worth of property values that the association is charged with maintaining and protecting, along with additional millions of dollars in common area assets and reserves.

The sense of community and responsibility that motivates homeowners to volunteer is essential to their living together in peace and harmony. A departure from the early years of community associations is a realization that reasonableness in applying rules leads to a stronger community spirit. This practice has become a priority of the community association industry, particularly in recent years.

Association boards of directors especially are encouraged to be reasonable in their decision making, including when dealing with rules enforcement, delinquency collection, or issues between or among neighbors. Everyone should understand that rules and regulations must change with the times to suit particular communities and that their purpose is to promote a better way of life and to protect the marketability of units.

This sense of community results in emotional equity, which is achieved not by increases in the real value of the property but by the perceived advantages of living in the community association. These advantages are individual in nature because the sense of community is founded on different sets of values for different persons.

Some homeowners, for example, build their emotional equity from the feeling of safety and security provided by the community association. Others receive emotional equity from the common interests and activities that are promoted within the community association.

Whatever the specific reason, community associations create and support a strong sense of community and its corresponding emotional equity. In doing so they foster among residents a deeper feeling of living in an appropriately desirable neighborhood. Inevitably, such increased desirability leads to greater demand for housing units that are in community associations that reflect a strong sense of community, which, in turn, leads to an actual increase in their property values.

As the industry expands its focus on continuing education programs for board members, homeowners, and community managers, it will accelerate their understanding of their interrelated roles and responsibilities. The result should help these stakeholders become more reasonable and responsive while addressing issues of mutual interest. Doing so will facilitate developing emotional equity in and the further success of community associations.

REAPING THE BENEFITS
OF PROFESSIONAL MANAGERS

An estimated 15–17 percent of community associations in the United States employ the services of professional management firms or of individual professional managers. The role of professional management is to advise and guide the board of directors to make the best policy decisions for the community association, and then to implement them. Managers do not make the policies or decisions, except when empowered to do so by the board.

In most cases, the board will create policy by making a decision, and then the management firm will work within that policy to achieve the board's desired results. A common example of this is the adopted annual budget for the community association and the contractual spending authority of the management firm. Once the board of directors approves the budget, the management firm can implement the expenditures that are within the spending authority authorized either by contract or as reflected in the budget. In certain cases, expenses that exceed the budget or the spending authority of the management company would require specific approval from the board.

Clearly, professional management firms offer great advantages to community associations. Boards consist mostly of volunteers who are untrained in operating community associations that essentially are multimillion-dollar nonprofit mutual benefit associations. As a trained, experienced professional, a manager is the best resource for the board to use to avoid "reinventing the wheel" or exceeding its authority.

Breadth of experience is also a factor: While most board members may be familiar with only one or two communities, professional managers may have experience with dozens of associations over many years. What's more, their companies may manage hundreds of associations whose experiences are a resource to draw from when advising the board. Most managers also belong to national or state trade associations that serve the association management industry. These organizations are another important resource for them, especially as they guide their boards in decision-making processes. Many of these trade associations provide not only formal education for managers and board members but also certifications and advanced designations for managers.

Realizing and accepting their awesome responsibilities causes principled, conscientious boards of directors to turn to professional management firms. By delegating day-to-day operating duties, they can focus on high-level actions such as policy-making and budgetary decisions. It also will give them more time to be responsive to their constituents and to welcome all opportunities to increase voluntary participation and to promote community spirit. This will improve not only the success of their community associations but also their outlook.

RESPONDING TO NEGATIVITY

Like any other industry, community association management has its critics. They should be heard, and their legitimate concerns should be resolved. In many cases the issues raised resulted in improvements for particular associations and sometimes for all. Too often, however, critics of community associations focus on a few specific negative issues while ignoring their positive impact. Whether related to media coverage, misconceptions, or generalizations, this negativity merits examination and response.

Media coverage

Community associations and their industry sometimes are portrayed negatively in the media, in blogs, and even in some state legislatures. Why? Misery makes headlines, and the sound of shrill voices echoes above reason. Scrutiny is prevalent in every part of our society, from government and education to philosophy and religion, and transparency is important. Some people, however, are driven to controversy and negativism, sometimes with no reasonable rationale. Contentment and prosperity do not sell newspapers or drive ratings.

When a misguided board, for example, in an effort to collect a debt owed to the rest of its members, foreclosed on an eighty-seven-year-old woman over past assessments due and a $25 fine, it became national news. Apparently the longtime homeowner was unaware that she was in jeopardy and had defaulted on her obligation to the community. A more conscientious board would have tried to assist her, rather than take the heavy-handed approach of seeking to foreclose.

The story generated national coverage after a media outlet used the circumstance to illustrate the inappropriate use of power. Media coverage of this and other similar examples should offer "lessons learned" to board members who should be as reasonable and compassionate as they are fair and consistent.

By comparison, the same media might simply ignore the story of the community association that helped its residents avoid foreclosure, donated money to help a resident in need, or donated time and space for a charitable event. The result, unfortunately, is that the public is subjected to sensationalized stories of past negative association incidents but not to their countless gestures of generosity, goodwill, and customer service.

When a three-alarm fire heavily damaged a nearby family-owned restaurant, for example, community association members came to the rescue. With little fanfare, they assisted the owners in numerous ways, including requesting and securing donations to rebuild the restaurant. Their responsiveness and effectiveness enabled the owners to reopen their establishment sooner than expected.

No one sought recognition for this organized effort, though the effort was noteworthy. The same is true of numerous other examples of association management leaders who have come to the rescue of victims of natural and other disasters ranging from fires to hurricanes. Extensive media coverage certainly was not expected, but it possibly could motivate others to engage in similar Good Samaritan activities. It also would offer justifiable positive coverage of wonderful community spirit.

Misperceptions

Much criticism about community associations reflects misperceptions about access to specific types of communities. Those who repeatedly assert, for example, that community associations are harbors of discrimination where residents can insulate themselves from undesirables are wrong. This could not be farther from reality.

The community association is one of the most open types of housing in existence. The barriers to entry are purely economic: A person either can or cannot afford to own a home in a particular association. There are no other barriers or restrictions (with certain exceptions for some forms of cooperative or age-restricted housing). No community association has raised assessments artificially or adopted biased qualifications as a means of exclusion.

Purchasing a home in an association is entirely an issue between the buyer and seller. Active adult and assisted living communities that restrict entry use marketing ploys designed to attract particular groups by offering inducements specific to their needs. Never, however, does the restriction involve illegal discrimination.

Rules enforcement

Other critics complain that boards of directors are power-hungry authoritarians who are provoked by managers, lawyers, and other professional advisers to enforce rules and covenants aggressively. This also could not be farther from reality. Board members are fiduciaries and strive diligently to improve the community for the members. They typically are hard-working volunteers elected by the members to represent their best interests within the parameters of the governing documents and state laws. Unfortunately, isolated examples of poor judgment are repeated extensively, almost developing a life of their own. The truth is, however, that those bad experiences serve as lessons learned for other board members and often preclude similar problems elsewhere.

As professional advisers, most managers are trained to seek the most nonconfrontational ways to comply with laws and governing documents and to advise the board that compromise, rather than punishment, may be the best approach to achieve its goals. As in any industry, there are exceptions, but these mirror the same exceptions typically existing in society and are neither unique nor amplified by the community association structure.

In contrast to criticism, community associations and their boards and managers have evolved over the last decade to offer a more reasonable approach to rules and covenant enforcement. Industry scholars and practitioners have spent almost twenty years focusing on best practices for living in harmony and building a strong sense of community, rather than focusing on the devices of enforcement.

Homeowner volunteer leadership and manager/professional educational opportunities are at an all-time high. Groups, management firms, and professional organizations now offer more and more easily accessible opportunities for education and dissemination of current industry knowledge and standards. Increased educational opportunities are yielding benefits for community association members, leaders, and industry professionals. The results are a more sensible approach to community building and rules enforcement that incorporates a strong sense of "reasonableness" and fairness.

Lack of information

Another unfair criticism is that homeowners are uneducated, unaware, and unknowledgeable about the specific restrictions and rules related to purchasing property in a community association. This may have been true thirty years ago, but today the purposes and specifics about how associations operate and the mutual benefits they provide are fairly common knowledge. What's more, many real estate companies offer their agents specialized educational programs that deal with the operations and the benefits of community associations. Finally, most states have disclosure laws that potential home buyers receive copies of the CC&Rs and bylaws; rules and regulations; association budget and collection policy; and all other relevant materials. If homeowners are unaware of the responsibilities of living in an association-managed community, it is likely to be because they decided not to read the extensive information provided to them.

Community associations are a prevalent form of housing, and virtually every buyer has knowledge about the requirements of living in one. Professionals in every advisory field are well versed about what it means to live in a community association.

Rather than being a deterrent, restrictions in a community association promote peace and harmony within the community and help all neighbors live together. Many people choose to live in a community association today partly because there are rules that help promote harmony.

Generalizations

Much criticism of community associations is anecdotal and not widespread or customary in the industry. Often it is based on a generalization that grew from specific circumstances. A closer inspection reveals, for example, that criticism commonly generated is about an individual board or individual manager who makes a poor decision or becomes disgruntled for some reason. This is really no different from any other industry or government or philanthropic organization. In fact, during challenging economic periods, actions open to criticism for those organizations tend to increase.

The opposite appears true in community associations, as evidenced by the strong belief of homeowners who trust in the actions of their elected board members and professional managers. The CAI Research Foundation study of 2009 shows that an overwhelming 89 percent of community association homeowners responded positively when asked if they thought their board members served the best interests of their communities as a whole. What's more, 76 percent responded that their managers provided value and support to residents and to the community as a whole.

Appropriate responses

Responding to criticism is appropriate in several ways: The truth must be told, and wrongs must be righted. When someone brings forth a problem, it should be resolved swiftly, fully, and fairly and should serve as a lesson learned from which to preclude recurrence. When a critic with an ulterior or unreasonable motive attacks the industry without justification or regard for the truth, he or she must be rebutted. Above all, community associations must increase their vigilance in identifying and resolving problems; responding to criticism; and paving a path toward better understanding, acceptance, and professionalism. Effective and honest communication is imperative in this regard.

DIFFERENTIATING
COMMUNITY ASSOCIATIONS

Community associations offer and provide different benefits for different homeowners and lifestyles. Location, price, and amenities often are cited as primary considerations by potential home buyers. The prospective homeowner may look at architecture, land characteristics, and even the quality of the local schools in deciding where to live. These attributes are not unique to the community association but are essential in the purchasing decision.

What differentiates community associations from other types of housing options and from other community associations is their ability to provide privacy, independence, and a sense of community. Equally, if not more, important is the universal concept of the association helping to protect the property values of homes within its boundaries.

A poignant example that personifies this concept is the annual Flower Day sponsored by an environmentally aware community. Each year its association purchases flowers that thrive in the soil and weather conditions and "gives" them to any community members who will plant them around their homes. This special event clearly brings people together while beautifying their homes and community. Indeed, Flower Day perfectly illustrates the value of shared cost and mutual benefit—all while building emotional and financial equity.

A well-run community association becomes coveted in a particular area. Its homes do not flood the real estate market because people want to stay in the neighborhood. Participation and the sense of community are strong in such successful associations.

Even foreclosures may be limited if home values remain above the average. In fact, experience dictates that, generally, higher emotional equity will increase demand and reduce supply. Both lead to higher property values and lower likelihood of foreclosures. It is quite clear that the successful, high-functioning community association improves the quality of life of its homeowners in a way that living in other neighborhoods cannot.

There may be some community associations that are not well run or high functioning, just as there are other housing neighborhoods with similar issues. Those are the exception, not the rule. In times of economic downturn when municipal governments are cutting staff and services to balance their budgets, the community association, run by volunteers, is positioned to be an increasingly attractive housing option.

Community association living is significantly different from the alternative. As more home buyers learn about its advantages, the demand will increase—and it will be met, probably sooner rather than later.

ADAPTING TO CHANGING ISSUES

Community associations can be responsive when dealing with changing issues. There are three examples that epitomize their adaptive nature.

The first pertains to the technological issue of satellite dishes. Many early condominium documents prohibited the installation of satellite dishes in the common areas. These were large satellite dishes that negatively impacted aesthetics and property values. Then technology changed, and small satellite dishes became common. They could be well hidden and would not impact either the common elements or the aesthetics of the neighborhood. Many community associations changed their documents to allow satellite dishes, while others created governance policies that permitted the dishes but required assurance that the homeowner retained responsibility for the dish. Still others understood that the aesthetic rules really applied only to the large satellite dishes and not to the new technology.

In the midst of the strong trend to adapt to the changing technology, new federal laws prohibited the ban of satellite dishes in community associations and other commercial properties, although certain restrictions were allowed. Today satellite dishes are prevalent in most community associations and are not aesthetic nightmares.

The second example relates to home-based businesses. While many community associations have rules governing residential use of homes, their intent was to prohibit commercial activities that would interfere with the "quiet enjoyment" of the neighborhood. Consequently, a homeowner could not open a retail business that required unreasonable traffic in the community.

Then came the advent of computer-based businesses and the growing interest and ability to work from home. Many associations amended or clarified their rules or governing documents to permit home-based businesses that do not infringe unreasonably on their neighbors' privacy. If they hadn't, the letter of the rule prohibiting home-based businesses would have been violated by those who could work quietly at their computers without bothering anyone—perhaps without anyone even knowing about it.

The third example pertains to displaying the American flag. From the beginning, governing documents commonly prohibited flag displays in community associations. When countless Americans reinvigorated their patriotism after the terrorist attack of 2001, community associations responded by relaxing this rule and permitting flag display.

Interestingly, if not incredibly, the patriotic act of flying the colors has been challenged in other arenas. Perhaps the most unusual example centers on a state senator who had to fight his Capitol Preservation Board to display his flag at the entrance to his office. Similarly, a resident at a public housing complex successfully demanded that the American flag be flown on the bare pole in the patio area. Both succeeded, but most would argue that their battles were unnecessary.

In each of these cases—satellite dishes, home-based businesses, and American flag display—legal judgments and new state laws eventually resulted in required rules changes. Nevertheless, the adaptive nature of the community association industry already was on its way to self-deregulation. Adapting to change is based on more than lessons learned; it is the hallmark of the modern association. It also is one of the underlying reasons for its bright future in American society and beyond.

CONCLUSION

Community associations have grown from meager beginnings to a viable and often preferred style of living. By meeting the needs and expectations of its homeowners, each community association can add value to their quality of life while adding worth to their property values.

Critics of community associations rely on either old or isolated attention-worthy abuses that tend to capture media attention. These cases are no more prevalent than would be found within any other group or population segment. What's more, survey research indicates that residents in association-managed communities are knowledge-able about their respective policies, are overwhelmingly satisfied living in a community association, and are pleased with their board members and their community managers. If they weren't, community associations would not be growing exponentially.

Community associations are here to stay. They are woven into the fabric of society, and their ability to adapt to changes in technology and to societal movements demonstrates their perseverance.

DAVID AND SANDRA
learn the value of mutually beneficial rules

Myth: Board members are dictators, and community managers are unreasonable.

Buster: Homeowners elect board members from among themselves, and all of them are eligible to run. If any board members act inap-propriately, they can be challenged at reelection time or removed by procedures outlined in the association's bylaws. Boards enforce the association's rules to protect and enhance the value of the community and its homes, and they operate from an informed, common sense perspective.

David and Sandra learned from experience that boards are reasonable and fair in enforcing rules to protect property values. David's career and the family were blossoming, and Sandra thrived as a work-at-home mom. With the kids a bit older and toys a lot larger, the family needed a bigger house and different amenities for entertaining. To accommodate their emerging needs, they bought a new home with its own swimming pool. It was nestled in a golf course community with a country club and tennis courts, and their new yard was big enough to practice soccer and enjoy grilling.

Because Sandra's experience with her last association was so good, she quickly began to volunteer around the community and was elected to its board of directors. One of her first challenges came fairly quickly. During the community manager's routine inspection, he noticed that a homeowner recently had completed a seven-foot fence. As far as fences go, it was beautiful, with triple-crown molding and custom arched doors.

The issue, technically, was that it was one foot taller than the governing documents allowed. This became a sticky situation for Sandra and the board. The fence actually helped beautify the community, but the homeowners had built the fence too tall, in part because they had not consulted with or gotten permission from the Architectural Review Committee before constructing it.

Sandra struggled with this because she was just starting to make friends with these neighbors and certainly didn't want to force them to alter their high-end fence just because of a rule in the governing documents. What was reasonable to do in this case? The board ultimately decided that its most important role was to protect the value of the community.

The height of the fence didn't matter as much as its type of wood, stain color, and ensuring that fence poles were inside versus outside—all of which were all proper in this case. Other homeowners didn't seem to mind that the fence was taller; it wasn't obstructing a view.

All things considered, the board made an exception and approved the fence. In the process, Sandra learned more about what it meant to be a leader in a thriving community. Counter to what she had heard about board members being dictators and managers being unreasonable, she joined her colleagues in behaving like reasonable elected representatives who considered the big picture and the best interests of homeowners while protecting their property values.

FREQUENTLY ASKED QUESTIONS

Q1: What has been the growth rate of community associations over the years?

A1: More than 62 million persons live in more than 314,200 community associations in the United States. This is a phenomenal growth rate, considering that in 1980 an estimated 9.6 million residents lived in 36,000 community associations; in 1990, 29.6 million residents lived in 130,000 associations; and by 2000, more than 45.2 million residents lived in 222,500 community associations. Clearly, this growth rate reflects the popularity of community associations and the satisfaction of its homeowners.

Q2: How will I know if a certain community association is right for me and my family?

A2: Affordability, proximity to local schools and other points of interest, churches, shopping, etc., are just some of the criteria you should consider. Additionally, you should assure yourself that the community passes the peace, tranquility, security, and financial tests discussed herein. Driving through the community and reviewing the governing documents and financial statements are an absolute must. If possible, talk to residents and other persons who are familiar with or have experience with a particular community association.

Q3: Is it difficult to make changes in a community association?

A3: As should be the case with any form of democratic governance, change is achievable by the majority. Outdated governing documents or rules can be amended, authoritarian board members can be voted out of office, and common amenities can be added, all by majority vote. The governing documents always contain provisions for change with the required threshold for a majority.

Q4: Why are there homeowners, instead of professionals, on the community association boards of directors?

A4: The nature of a community association affords the homeowners the right and obligation to participate in a democratic form of self-governance. Their volunteerism has been and will be an essential component for the success of their community association. Because of the immense responsibility, knowledge, and skills required to manage multimillion-dollar properties, it also is prudent for community associations to hire professional management firms to guide and implement board decisions.

Q5: Where can I get a copy of the Zogby Study that was done for the Research Foundation of the CAI?

A5: Copies of the 2009 Zogby Study can be requested from the CAI via CAIOnline.org or 703-548-8600. Their surveys in 2005 and 2007 produced very similar results: All three indicated that homeowners are very positive about the community association way of life.

PART II

IMPROVING

COMMUNITY

ASSOCIATIONS

CHAPTER 4

How to Improve Community Associations through Education

Education is the ability to listen to almost anything
without losing your temper or your self-confidence.

—ROBERT FROST
American poet

INTRODUCTION

The business of community associations requires numerous participants who can interact productively for their mutual benefit. When challenges arise, those who are educated with the appropriate knowledge and skills are most likely to excel. Accordingly, dealing with issues swiftly and effectively should be part of an evolving learning process that is essential to improving community associations. That process must include all who provide services to associations and all who benefit from them.

Continuing education is the single most important way to improve community associations. This is true of short-term as well as of long-term improvements. Homeowners and home buyers must know and understand thoroughly their responsibilities as members, just as board members, managers, and other professionals must understand theirs as leaders and service providers. All of them also must know and understand the mutual benefits of protecting property values while nurturing and developing community spirit.

What's more, armed with appropriate knowledge and skills, they can enhance their effectiveness not only in resolving conflict but also in precluding or minimizing it. If truly educated, they will reflect Robert Frost's standards by being able to listen to varying degrees of negativity without losing their temper or self-confidence.

Interestingly, most, if not all, disputes in community associations are caused by lack of information, communication, and understanding—often the result of lack of education. Noted community association lawyer and pioneer, Wayne Hyatt, may have described this best in *Community First!*, edited by Bill Overton:

> One of the primary causes of disharmony in community associations is the buyer who does not understand the regulations and procedures, including the role of the board of directors, at the time of purchase. This can be compounded by inadequate training of board members. Too often neither the association members nor the candidates for the board understand what qualities make good board members, what the director may and may not do . . . The result is a loss of positive opportunity and, more seriously, the presence of a combative environment and governance problems.

Resolving this situation while improving community associations requires offering continuing education to homeowners, potential home buyers, board members, real estate agents, managers, and other professionals. Clearly, community associations can be improved by developing custom-tailored, easily accessible short courses for these targeted participants. Great strides have been made in this direction and, obviously, more should be made. Only through education will all stakeholders understand more vividly the responsibilities, expectations, and benefits of association living. That is the premise of this chapter.

EDUCATING HOMEOWNERS

Without question, continuing education for everyone involved in the day-to-day affairs of a community association is the most important means of improving community associations. Cumulatively, home-owners should demand a community association that provides an impeccably maintained property, peace and harmony, and a sound fiscal program. To realize that ideal, quality education must be available readily to everyone involved in the community association process.

The importance of educating homeowners is step one in the process. Although some may have lived in a community association previously, for many it is a first-time experience. Their sellers may have shared some insight into their new way of life, but many buyers do not read the governing documents carefully before making their purchasing decision.

What's more, they tend to focus more on the advantages of community association living while ignoring the related responsibilities. By participating in short courses designed especially for them and developed and offered for their convenience, homeowners can increase their understanding, maximize their effective voluntary participation, and enhance their happiness.

Three neighbors with varying degrees of interest in maintaining their yards illustrate the impact of association rules. While one was devoted to making his yard beautiful, the second struggled to meet minimal standards, and the third often was cited for violations. Without the community association's rules, two of the three yards might have become deplorable, negatively impacting property values and aesthetics in the immediate neighborhood. Because of effective enforcement, however, the neighbors complied, although one did so begrudgingly, thereby protecting the value of their homes.

When homeowners understand that rules are intended to protect and enhance property values and to serve the greater good, they are more likely to abide by them. If they realize that outdated rules can be updated through the democratic process, they may be motivated to serve on committees or on the board of directors. As they master all aspects of model homeownership, they are more likely to participate in the association and less likely to be apathetic or disgruntled.

Although some board members and managers may prefer apathy to resistance, indifference eventually results in problems. Frankly, homeowners who don't care enough to read and understand their association's financial statements, and board members who don't care whether they do, are asking for trouble. If, for example, a community association has financial challenges, it is imperative that the board and management articulate the issues, explain the causes, and provide alternative solutions. Ongoing education about the importance of reading and understanding the association's financials should empower all concerned to help preclude problems and to collaborate in resolving them if and when they arise.

Generally, good homeowners are good neighbors who develop emotional equity not only in their homes but also in their communities. They understand that, like friendship, neighborliness is a two-way street. Equally important, they support policies and rules created for the "greater good" and promote peace and harmony. Such positive attitudes are imperative in community associations because, together, homeowners can protect and enhance their property values and improve the quality of each other's lives. This is a responsibility that includes adhering to the governing documents, including when they might be inconvenient.

The best homeowners in community associations also participate in their self-governance process. They enjoy the sponsored activities, serve on committees, attend board and annual meetings, and might even consider running for the board of directors. If they disagree with a rule, they offer a constructive alternative and work through the process to get it changed.

Above all, they are mindful of their neighbors and strive to make homeownership in their community association a joy for all. These opportunities should be explained to potential home buyers. Alternatively, they should be highlighted in ongoing efforts to educate homeowners. Members who are highly educated about their association's purpose and potential typically are the happiest and participate most.

The best time to begin educating homeowners is when a community is being developed. The most successful and visionary developers ensure that their new homeowners receive initial education about their governing documents and communities at the time they close their purchases. Equally important, while the community association is under their control, these developers name new homeowners to their boards of directors.

Those who are authorized by state laws and governing documents to retain a majority of board members while sales of their homes continue should allow homeowners to serve with them in a minority role. This is important for purposes of transition and harmony. It also serves as highly educational and valuable "on-the-job training" for future board members elected by homeowners after they assume control of the board. Given experience, they should be more successful in governing the affairs of their community associations.

Unquestionably, educated homeowners are more likely to be constructive. After all, how can they abide by the rules or try to change them if they don't know them? That is why potential homeowners should read the governing documents of an association before deciding whether to live there. The wide array of communities means buyers are likely to find one in which they will live happily and participate productively. Educated homeowners, like educated board members, will result in community associations improving at a much faster pace.

EDUCATING HOME BUYERS

The need to educate homeowners is steeped in the need to educate potential home buyers. Educating home buyers about community association living before they decide to buy will lessen the urgency to educate homeowners later. Stellar community managers and boards of directors understand this, and others should follow their example.

Educational efforts definitely should target potential home buyers in established community associations and especially in their newly developing counterparts. The prepurchase disclosure information potential buyers receive from the association and the seller should provide insight into their new ways of life and specifics about their community associations. Generally, however, this information is voluminous, difficult to comprehend, and mentioned only in passing. Seldom, if ever, is it as useful as it should be in educating the potential association member. Clearly, further education is needed, and improvements must be made.

The effort to educate potential buyers should include an explanation of the varied responsibilities and advantages of living in different kinds of associations. Living in a gated community comprising single-family homes, for example, differs drastically from living in a high-rise condominium. Buyers will be happiest when they buy the most suitable unit for their budgets, lifestyles, and preferences. Not being fully educated about the associations they choose can cause problems and result in unnecessary unhappiness later.

Consider the case of a married doctoral student who left home for a year of residency studies and rented an apartment in a complex outside an association. Located by a beautiful lake, the building attracted undergraduates who partied incessantly, often through early morning hours, precluding her studying and sleeping.

Worried about her grades and health, she moved to an association-managed condominium at the end of the semester. She enthusiastically welcomed the rules that prohibited loud music, hammering, and even using dishwashers or clothes washers after ten p.m. Those rules may have seemed onerous to others, but this renter embraced them. She learned about their benefits through experience and found a more suitable place where owners and renters placed a premium on late-night peace and quiet.

Although a renter and not a buyer, the tenant benefited from understanding the governing documents that bound her and her landlord. She reaped the benefits of educating herself about community associations.

As her needs and purposes changed through the years following her graduation, she rented four different condos as second homes—all in community associations. The doctor wouldn't have it any other way!

The lessons learned through these experiences are applicable to home buyers. Given the great variety of choices, they are likely to find a community association that is suitable for them. A wise decision means finding one with governing documents that are consistent with their preferences.

One of the best ways to improve community associations is for their boards of directors and managers to ensure that home buyers are educated fully before they make their purchasing decision and then to supplement their learning through an ongoing effort. In doing so they also could be educating future members of the committee or the board of directors.

Developing and offering short courses and informational materials for potential home buyers would be a wise course of action for board members and managers. Topics should include the buying process, the rationale for rules and regulations related to living in a particular association, and governing aspects.

Ensuring that new members embrace all aspects of their selected community associations certainly would help them build emotional equity in their homes and neighborhoods. The best management companies are doing this already, hoping to set an industry trend that will benefit all associations and their residents.

EDUCATING BOARD MEMBERS

Board members are another important group requiring education. Responsible for governing their communities, they are charged by their governing documents to maintain and enhance their common facilities. This includes their responsibility to maintain the property and to levy and collect assessments.

Their overall task is not easy: to operate like a business, act like a government, and promote community spirit. The board therefore must have at its disposal the same caliber of education offered to other industry professionals. This means educating board members first and foremost to understand their responsibilities and expectations and, second but equally important, to master the qualities of leadership and tools necessary to achieve their goals.

Mike Vance, the creator of Disney University and the Creative Thinking Institute, defines leadership as "the ability to establish standards and manage a creative climate where people are self-motivated toward the mastery of long-term constructive goals in a participatory environment of mutual respect compatible with personal values." His definition applies perfectly to the leadership role of a community association board. All the powers of a board to levy assessments, enforce the CC&Rs, and promulgate rules and regulations target their basic responsibility of protecting the value of the assets. There is no other reason to assign such powers to boards.

To meet the need for adequate training, successful community association management companies provide at least cursory board orientation courses that define the board's responsibilities. Some go so far as to offer interrelated customized orientation courses not only for board members but also for committee members, homeowners, and managers. Developed in consultation with experts in communication, education, and leadership, these courses are offered online, in traditional face-to-face settings, and in published and electronic formats.

Admittedly, sometimes even the best training does not have the desired results. An accomplished trainer, for example, conducted a one-day parliamentary procedure and effective meeting skills workshop for quarreling board members plagued by personality conflicts in a large self-managed condominium association.

Although the tension among them persisted, board members enthusiastically agreed to embrace basics such as using a gavel, a timed agenda, and parliamentary procedure. They even agreed to limit discussion and to prohibit discussion or conversation without a motion on the floor.

Invited to observe their next meeting, the trainer was dismayed to see them march into the meeting room in single file, like soldiers! Looking deadly serious, they seemed to be sizing up the crowd and each other.

Finally, one of them said, "Mr. President, I move to say hello."

The president responded, "There is a motion to say hello. Is there a second?"

After several seconds of absolute silence, the president banged his gavel and announced, "The motion died for lack of a second." No one was allowed to say hello.

Clearly, these board members needed continuing education—and perhaps a professional manager who could help them resolve their differences and conduct more efficient and productive meetings.

Some states are at the forefront of requiring continuing education for community association boards of directors. Florida, for example, offers a 2.5-hour certification course for association board members and requires them to sign an affirmation that they have read and understand the governing documents for their respective community associations. Hawaii sets aside money every year for the education of community association board members by third-party providers, which can include CAI and the Maui Condominium Council.

Given the economic stakes, everyone involved in the community association management industry should encourage greater board member participation in targeted continuing education programs. Association members should expect every board member to take advantage of the many training opportunities available throughout the year in virtually every market.

Spending two or three hours at the beginning of every year to hold a board orientation and training program seems like a small commitment of time, given the value of the assets every board is charged to protect.

The best management companies encourage board members to participate in training programs continually. Whether provided online, in group settings, or via electronic or written materials, the range of information is as varied as board members' needs and interests. Of particular note is their emphasis on reasonableness, fairness, and compassion. Any misguided board member who craves authority and cannot wait to wield a gavel must learn immediately the hallmarks of effective representation.

Educating board members is a wise course of action that is likely to reap benefits for all concerned. It is a worthy goal that should be embraced by all associations.

EDUCATING REALTORS®

Education is the key to ensuring that all who serve community associations understand their responsibilities. This group comprises not only homeowners, board members, and managers but also Realtors®, attorneys, Certified Public Accountants, Reserve Specialists®, and many other professionals and vendors. The ideal community necessitates their meeting their responsibilities professionally. Their doing so is essential to improving community associations.

Realtors® and their associates comprise an especially important group of professionals who require an in-depth understanding of community associations. As the first point of contact that a potential unit owner may have with a community association, all real estate agents must understand and explain appropriately the detailed elements of this type of living. Specifically, through education and information exchange they should ascertain that potential home buyers are educated fully and appropriately about the intricacies of living in an association-managed community. They should help their customers understand how governing documents bind homeowners and the association and how they would be impacted by a particular set of CC&Rs, bylaws, and rules.

This is supremely important because those who understand the advantage of living under rules that benefit all and will protect and enhance property values are likely to thrive as neighbors. Those who object to the regulations, powers of the board, and the mutual responsibilities and assessments involved in successful community associations might prefer to live elsewhere.

A wonderful example of educating Realtors® was set in the Upper Midwest by an association that rented and operated a booth at a convention of the local Board of Realtors®. The manager and several board members of this mid-rise downtown property spent the day there, distributing color brochures, explaining the benefits of living in their community, and promoting their outreach to Realtors®. Above all, the association's astute manager emphasized the sales-friendly board's priority of assisting real estate agents in the responsible sale of units in the community.

The return on this investment of time and energy was impressive: stronger, mutually beneficial, and productive relationships with like-minded professionals. Most important, this short-term educational effort prepared local Realtors® to educate their clients about the advantages of buying homes in this community.

Continuing education programs also will help Realtors® work more successfully with associations by complying with their policies during the sales process. Many communities, for example, have covenants or rules governing signage and guest parking. Agents who work with associations will realize they have powerful allies to help sell listings. Education will help them understand the intricacies of community associations and strengthen their abilities to articulate the advantages and responsibilities of ownership to potential home buyers.

Minnesota is among the states that recognize and offer continuing education credits for Realtors® who complete approved courses relating to community associations. Many others are considering doing so as well—and they should.

EDUCATING COMMUNITY ASSOCIATION MANAGERS

The importance of professionally trained managers cannot be overestimated. Managing a community association is a very complex business. The areas of expertise required are likely to exceed even the collective knowledge and experience of board members. In fact, the community association management profession grew out of a need expressed by volunteer board members for help, guidance, and property management skills that they lacked or simply did not have time to perform. As the professional management industry emerged and matured over time, it developed into a specialty all its own. The skills required to manage community associations include the following:

> Read and explain financial statements.

> Create and explain multimillion-dollar budgets with multiple components.

> Negotiate with vendors from multiple disciplines.

> Create, modify, analyze, and explain multiple bids about a wide variety of projects.

> Possess working knowledge of property management, including inspections involving a wide variety of construction and capital elements of the property.

> Exhibit high-level oral and writing communication skills, excelling in managing group dynamics, addressing board and annual meetings, and reporting to boards of directors.

> Communicate with, inspire, and work with volunteers who may serve in many different roles in a community.

> Reflect deep knowledge of rules, policies, and procedures that have proved successful for other associations.

> Understand the governing documents of the community association.

> Have a working knowledge of collection laws and procedures.

> Understand federal and state laws that impact the operations of community associations in particular states.

> Read and understand technical manuals and specifications about subjects ranging from HVAC and air-exchange systems in high-rise buildings to the care and maintenance of ponds, lakes, golf courses, and other relevant topics.

> Excel in essential skills such as developing a management action plan and reserve study.

This is by no means a comprehensive list of the skills required to manage community associations successfully. In fact, it would be impossible to identify all of the requirements because they are evolving. The challenge facing professional community managers today involves the shifting legal requirements that must be met by associations and their boards, as well as the evolving ancillary professions that assist managers in informing boards about their legal and fiduciary responsibilities.

Policies that may have been effective last year may need to be modified this year. Insurance standards, building codes, election procedures for boards, towing requirements, ability to levy assessments or fines, banking regulations, and resale disclosure requirements, among many others, can change every year. It is becoming increasingly difficult for volunteer board members to keep pace with the ever-evolving legal landscape regarding the operation of their communities. This is precisely why they turn to professional managers for assistance.

But how do managers stay current with all the changes taking place? Perpetual training and education are the answer. Professional community managers usually receive hands-on training supervised by their management companies and hold advanced certifications or designations that reflect their levels of expertise. Florida and Nevada require community managers to be licensed, and the California Association of Community Managers offers a manager certification program. The CAI also offers a national certification program and the advanced Professional Community Association Manager designation, which is the highest achievement in association management recognized anywhere in the world.

It seems unlikely today, and certainly in the future, that managers who are uneducated and untrained in the specialty of community association management will be able to offer much or any useful advice to their clients. The complexities and challenges of managing multimillion-dollar not-for-profit corporations will overwhelm the uneducated and unprepared.

Only managers who have dedicated themselves to mastering the diverse multilevel disciplines required to assist their clients effectively will be ready to succeed. They will do so by working hand-in-hand with volunteers elected to lead those corporations. Together they must nurture and promote a strong sense of community to help protect their community's property values. Clearly, improving community associations begins with educating their community managers.

EDUCATING OTHER PROFESSIONALS

Numerous professionals work with community associations, providing services ranging from legal and accounting to building and restoring. Although some have skills that are applicable to any industry, others must learn to meet the specific needs and requirements of associations. To meet this demand, the CAI offers excellent education programs leading to certification and/or designation programs for attorneys, accountants, insurance agents, and reserve specialists. Law schools such as the California Western School of Law in San Diego offer real estate courses that include a focus on community associations.

Certifications and designations are meaningful because meeting their requirements is challenging. To receive a CAI designation, for example, a Reserve Specialist® must demonstrate competency by preparing at least thirty reserve studies; hold a bachelor degree in construction management, architecture, or engineering (or equivalent experience and education); and comply with strict rules of conduct.

No one said that continuing education was easy or inexpensive. It is, however, an investment that yields benefits not only for those who are educated but also for their customers. The community association industry can improve itself significantly by providing perpetual training for its personnel and for those whom they serve. The best companies have a strong course of action for accomplishing such important continuing education goals.

CONCLUSION

The community association process is complicated. Just as "a chain is as strong as its weakest link," so are community associations. The key to improving associations is education for homeowners, home buyers, board members, managers, Realtors®, and other appropriate professionals.

The industry must take the lead in meeting the need for improvement in all areas of responsibility. This is its fiduciary duty, and leaders at all levels will embrace this goal if they are to improve at the pace they should and must. Together stakeholders, including homeowners, municipalities, managers, and developers, can develop a cohesive mindset to improve community association living while achieving peace, harmony, and security along the path started many years ago.

DAVID AND SANDRA
benefit from homeowner training

Myth: Homeowners are not interested in helping to run the community.

Buster: Homeowners want to be involved, especially when home-owner education programs show them how to participate effectively.

David and Sandra learned how board members and committee members voluntarily can contribute their time, energy, and talent to serve their neighbors. Now parents of teenagers, they still loved their home and their community. Soon after Sandra was elected board president, their community experienced weeks of hot, dry weather. The weeks turned into months, and still there was no rain in the forecast.

Just as the community was experiencing this situation, the community manager suggested that the board offer a homeowner training seminar about water conservation and effective landscaping for dry climates. Sandra and her fellow board members agreed. The training turned out to be quite informational and well attended. To create excitement for the event, the board recruited local vendors to attend and to sponsor demonstrations and products from their businesses.

Participating homeowners were armed with great water-saving tips that they could use in and around their homes. They also learned how selecting drought-tolerant plants for their home flowerbeds could help ensure water savings going forward. The training sparked a lively discussion among homeowners and their community manager about how the information could be applied in the association's common areas. After all, water conservation is good for the environment and good for the community's financial well-being.

Based on this interaction, the board appointed a homeowners committee to consider the issue and conduct a survey. Based on the recommendations of these volunteers, they voted unanimously to undertake a complimentary comprehensive water usage audit with a well-known landscaping services vendor.

Homeowners enjoyed participating in the process, especially because the landscaping eventually saved their community precious resources and thousands of dollars in water usage. Sandra and the board learned from experience that homeowners welcomed opportunities to volunteer to serve their communities on committees and even on the board, especially when education and training were provided. Given the opportunity, they enjoy helping to run the community.

FREQUENTLY ASKED QUESTIONS

Q1: I am a Realtor® and would like to take a course about community associations. What are my options?

A1: Many states have accredited continuing education opportunities regarding community associations. If yours does not, work through your board of Realtors® to encourage the appropriate state officials to explore possibilities with real estate schools and/or community association management companies. If your state does not have a department of real estate, direct initial inquiries to the secretary of state or other appropriate agency.

Q2: I am a new homeowner in a community association. Although our real estate agent reviewed the CC&Rs, bylaws, and rules with my husband and me before our purchase, we do not understand some of their provisions. Where can we get help?

A2: Your plight is very common but can be resolved easily. You have several alternatives. Feel free to approach your association manager or board of directors for advice. Ask if they can answer your questions or whether you should speak at the next open forum of the board or can participate in a homeowner education course. Other homeowners may have the same interest. If so, the board could schedule a meeting at which they, the manager, or an attorney could review the governing documents and answer questions from interested homeowners.

Continuing education opportunities for homeowners are as essential as those for board members, managers, and other professionals. Understanding the governing documents well can enhance your success within the association.

Q3: How can I trust our board of directors to be knowledgeable enough to manage our multimillion-dollar property wisely?

A3: Your board of directors has a fiduciary duty to manage the association's property wisely. To accomplish this, boards usually hire management companies that provide the advice and support needed to implement their policies, decisions, and directives. Homeowners have access to financial reports and other materials related to their performance, so they can judge for themselves.

The best management companies offer orientation and continuing education training programs that enable board members to do a better job in protecting property values.

Q4: I am worried about buying a home in a community association and then finding out too late that it has oppressive rules that are impossible to follow. What can I do to preclude that?

A4: Rest assured that you will have every opportunity to review the governing documents, including the rules, of any community association in which you are considering buying a home. Homeowners who are surprised typically are those who didn't take the time to read and to understand them.

Your priority should be to find a home in a community association that has rules that are compatible with your lifestyle. If you favor midnight swims and late-night weekday pool parties, for example, you won't want to live in a condominium that closes the pool at nine p.m.

Your Realtors® and your local board of Realtors® should have brochures about community association living. If you have a particular community in mind, however, you can get information that pertains specifically to it from your Realtors® or from the appropriate management company. If your state has a department of real estate, it should have brochures, too.

Q5: I am serving on a community association board of directors. How do I go about finding a reputable community association management company?

A5: Referrals from other community association boards are the best approach to finding a reputable community association management company. Your board's success will be enhanced by selecting an experienced company that offers quality continuing education for its boards of directors, managers and staff, prospective and current homeowners, Realtors®, and appropriate professionals.

CHAPTER 5

How to Improve Community Associations through Performance

There will always be a tension between the needs of the
individual and the needs of the group. Both must be honored.

—JOHN W. GARDNER

Presidential Medal of Freedom Recipient

INTRODUCTION

Excellence in customer service depends on exceeding customers'
expectations through impressive performance. The best companies
in every industry understand that problems will occur and that they
should be resolved immediately and satisfactorily. As John Gardner
noted, the needs of individuals and of groups must be honored in
resolving conflict.

Tensions between individuals and groups that comprise community associations are inevitable, and they must be identified, addressed,
and resolved—never ignored or denied. Dealing with them swiftly
and effectively should be part of a perpetually evolving process that is
essential to improving community associations.

Today's community associations differ dramatically from their
predecessors not only in number but also in scope, services, strategies, and philosophy. Criticisms of the past have served as lessons
learned that are the basis for better customer service. No one claims

that community associations are perfect; no living environment is. What professionals rightfully claim, however, is that contemporary associations are committed to improvement in protecting property values while providing a better quality of life.

Much has changed since the first modern condominium association was developed in Salt Lake City in 1960. More than one thousand years ago, however, the first community association in the United States was built in northern New Mexico, namely, the Taos Pueblo. With its common walls and common facilities, the pueblo remains occupied to this day. Like other modern community associations, it is governed by a council elected by members of the community.

Blessed with a rich history, the Taos and other pueblos in the southwest have been influential in many regards, including in their stamp on southwestern architecture. Their continuous existence is proof that community association living meets the needs of its members, especially as it evolves over time. It could not have succeeded without continuously improving itself while adapting to changing needs and interests and improving its performance.

Indeed, community associations have changed significantly over the past ten decades. To reach their potential in terms of their social and economic core, however, they will need to change even more. The questions are, how should they change, how can they improve, and what lies ahead? The answers portend the future and reflect the aphorism that "the ship that never changes course has a fool for a captain."

These sweeping generalizations are the basis from which to identify specific areas in which community associations can improve their performance. They also are the basic steps along the pathway toward reaching that goal. Although opportunities for improvement are highlighted throughout this book, this chapter will focus on how to improve an association's performance by improving its board of directors, board meetings, and measurements of success.

IMPROVING COMMUNITY ASSOCIATION BOARDS OF DIRECTORS

Improving community association boards of directors first requires understanding their responsibilities. From the beginning of the community association movement in the United States, practitioners have debated whether a community association is more of a quasi-government focused on building a sense of community or simply a not-for-profit corporation with millions of dollars in assets. In other words, is it a mini-government or a business enterprise operating a multimillion-dollar not-for-profit corporation? Alternatively, is it a hybrid? The answer requires examining the responsibilities of the association to its members. These include protection of assets, fiduciary obligations, and delegation of authority.

Protection of assets

Nearly every professional in the industry and most experienced volunteer practitioners agree that the overriding responsibility of the community association board of directors is to create policies and operate the association in a way that will "maintain, protect, and enhance" the value of the assets of the members.

Understanding the scope of this responsibility begins with considering the perspective of homeowners and how the value of the assets might be determined. For most association members, their homes are the largest investments they will ever make. For their emotional and financial security, it is important, especially in a market of diminishing values, that both the board and the members have a common understanding and constructive dialogue regarding these concepts and values.

For purposes of example, consider an association that has thirty-seven single-family homes with average individual values of approximately $225,000:

$225,000 × 37 = $8,325,000 total real estate assets,

plus $500,000 in reserves = $8,825,000 in total assets

This example illustrates that even a modestly sized community association can comprise enormous value. By comparison, the board of an association that has one hundred units with an average home value of $300,000 would manage a multimillion-dollar not-for-profit corporation with assets of approximately $30 million, plus reserves and cash on hand. Apply this equation to large-scale associations of one thousand units or more, and the numbers become stratospheric.

Home values and reserves, however, are only part of the equation. To understand the real meaning of value in a community association, consider another formula:

Value = curb appeal + the perception
of the quality of life by the members

In this formula, curb appeal refers to the location, amenities, landscaping, architecture of the buildings, maintenance of the property, and the value of the bricks and sticks. The perception of the quality of life is trickier.

Even in extremely well-maintained communities the value of properties can be diminished by comparison to others. Nothing sells real estate in a community association like word of mouth. If members of a community are happy living there, they will take pride in telling friends from larger communities how wonderful life is in their association. By contrast, if they feel that their communities are too restrictive or too lax, that they do not promote interaction among neighbors, or that their boards do not communicate well, they are likely to tell friends that they dislike living there and cannot wait to move out.

Indeed, a community association in a perfect location and in impeccable physical condition can suffer diminished values if homeowners' criticisms spread quickly to local real estate agents or to the media. The perception that an association is not necessarily a wonderful place to live may prompt sellers to show clients properties in other associations first. To retain value, every association must be impeccably maintained in accordance with its professional maintenance standards and ensure that the majority of members are enjoying life in the community.

Over the years, for example, developers built tens of thousands of associations with beautiful green spaces and common areas with wonderful amenities like parks and pools. Some whose beautiful amenities were all but abandoned because of onerous use restrictions also may have had trouble finding volunteers to serve on the board or on committees.

Why? Well-intended but untrained volunteers who misunderstood both the purpose and the mechanics of serving on an association board created policies and rules that inhibited the enjoyment of their communities. Sadly, this, in turn, impacted perceptions about the quality of life and possibly diminished property values. As community association leaders learned the hard way, however, these issues were resolved as reasonableness prevailed.

Homeowners may have certain expectations about their selected community and its lifestyle, neighborly interaction, and culture—all of which are established and nurtured by the board and its policies. The very first thing members should expect is that the policies of the board will protect the value of their homes by creating a friendly, welcoming, and enjoyable environment to live in and a maintenance standard for the common areas that will ensure its appeal to members and prospective buyers.

Sometimes board members truly conduct themselves in amazingly impressive ways. In a large mixed-use community association in the Southeast, for example, homeowners rose to the challenge when the developer went bankrupt and left them with a foreclosed property, $73.48 in the bank account, and an ugly grey hole in the ground that was supposed to be a swimming pool and clubhouse.

Homeowners elected a board of directors that negotiated with the bank and began to reconstruct their community. Led by a president who was an attorney and a treasurer who was a hospital CFO, determined board members and other homeowners volunteered their time, approved special assessments, and accepted a loan from a generous homeowner.

Within months, the board accumulated $46,663.62 in the bank; within two years, it completed the swimming pool and clubhouse. The association also reconstructed a beautiful front entrance and commissioned a physical needs assessment and capital reserve study.

This is the perfect example of the dedicated volunteers who give their time to serve on boards of directors and commit themselves to protecting their communities' assets. Over the years, homeowners have learned to expect this high standard of excellence from their elected board members.

They also expect the board to conduct its business in a businesslike way. Reports about chaotic, inappropriately informal, or unnecessarily lengthy board meetings may discourage prospective members of associations. They simply will not instill confidence that an association is run in a businesslike way that will protect the home values.

In fact, if it sounds like chaos, it probably is. Prospective members and board members alike should understand that property values are protected when board members conduct themselves in businesslike ways, especially at meetings; act in a fiduciary capacity while protecting the members' interests as if they were the personal interests of the board; and act lawfully and ethically at all times.

Because emotional equity is so clearly associated with property values for homeowners and home buyers, board members should encourage members to participate in the association's governance. By widely publicizing board meetings and homeowners annual meetings, for example, they can increase attendance. This means doing much more than posting the obligatory notices. It means using every available means to publicize meetings.

When board members are trained and understand their roles and responsibilities, most homeowners will feel freer to interact with them and to enjoy their neighbors and amenities. Empowering board members to understand the importance of meeting their responsibilities and the impact of their behavior and decisions is critical to protecting property values and quality of life. Doing so is critical to improving community associations.

Fiduciary obligation to members

A community association board of directors has a fiduciary duty to association members, an obligation that generally is defined by loyalty and full disclosure to them. Although fiduciary duties vary by state and with the type of relationship, the following general duties are listed in Michol O'Connor's *Texas Causes of Action*:

> › duty of loyalty and utmost good faith

> › duty of candor

> › duty to refrain from self-dealing, which extends to dealings with a fiduciary's spouse, agents, employees, and other persons whose interests are closely identified with those of the fiduciary

> › duty to act with integrity of the strictest kind

> › duty of fair, honest dealing and

> › duty of full disclosure.

Board members are in positions of trust from which they must represent homeowners and place their interests before their own. As fiduciaries they must always act in the best interests of members to "maintain, protect, and enhance" the value of their assets.

Board members who violate this position of trust may expose themselves to personal liability, even though they are acting as members of a board of directors of a corporation. Wise fiduciaries also abide by the "business judgment rule." In its simplest form this means association board members must practice the following:

> act in good faith

> practice fair dealing

> act within the limits of the directors' expertise and

> act lawfully and with ethical intent.

Acting in good faith simply means that board members will act in the interest of association members and will disclose fully any pertinent information and any potential conflicts of interest or potential self-enrichment. Fair dealing means that board members will disclose what they know about any given topic when they know it. In other words, they will not withhold information, spring surprises on the board or manager, and/or play "gotcha" with fellow board members, professionals who work for the association, or homeowners. Instead, information should be disclosed fully and timely to all concerned.

One of the most important elements of effective board service and of the business judgment rule is for board members to act within the limits of their expertise. Most board members are not chemists, agronomists, engineers, architects, roofing experts, insurance brokers or agents, lawyers, horticulturists, carpenters, contractors, paint manufacturers, etc.

They regularly must, however, review proposals and make decisions about specifications and contracts that include landscape maintenance, roofing and siding projects, painting projects, road and parking lot resurfacing, pest control, and insurance. Without expertise, how can they possibly, with any credibility, singlehandedly offer opinions and make decisions reviewing specifications and awarding contracts in these areas? The answer is simple: They cannot and should not.

Like any other board of directors of any other corporation, community association boards need to depend on the advice and guidance of outside experts. Board members must identify and realize the limits of their expertise in these areas and solicit the opinions of professionals.

Associations that are professionally managed can rely on their managers to gather required information, review the information with the experts, and report their findings as appropriate. The board should rely on the manager as one of the most powerful experts at its disposal.

After receiving advice from designated experts, especially from their professional managers, board members would be well advised to take that advice rather than second-guessing it and substituting their unskilled, untrained amateur opinions for those of trained, licensed professionals. In that way they will fulfill their fiduciary obligation to association members and comply with the business judgment rule.

If a professional's advice is wrong or if workmanship proves faulty, a board will have recourse against that professional. If, on the other hand, board members substitute their judgment for that of the professional by amending specifications or a contract to save money or cut corners against the advice of a professional, they will have exceedingly limited recourse if problems occur.

The fourth element of the business judgment rule highlights the importance of acting lawfully and ethically. In creating policy and making decisions, board members are bound legally by their association's hierarchy of authority.

It is useful to think of this hierarchy as a pyramid with federal laws at the top, followed downward successively by state statutes relating to community associations and not-for-profit corporations; municipal laws and codes; and a community association's Articles of Incorporation, CC&Rs, bylaws, and rules and regulations.

Board members always should comply with these legal requirements and with the highest ethical standards. They are bound to place the interest of members before their own. Under no circumstances should they attempt to benefit themselves, their families, or their friends, especially while awarding contracts or scheduling maintenance.

Those who have expertise in an area such as law or landscaping may express their informed opinions about a related subject. Their advice, however, cannot be considered the advice of professionals in their fields, unless a board hires and compensates them for that purpose. If this were to happen, they would have to recuse themselves from discussions regarding matters for which they were hired and then report and offer opinions acting as outside experts. This would be a chancy proposition at best.

The bottom line for the board is to hire professionals to create specifications, analyze bids, report their recommendations to the board—and then to take their advice.

Fiduciary obligations are serious matters. By ensuring that homeowners and board members understand their importance, community associations also can ensure that they meet their related standards. They can improve their performance by internalizing these principles and by abiding by them daily. Above all, they continuously must reflect loyalty to homeowners and full disclosure.

Delegation of authority

The board may delegate all of its authority but none of its responsibility. It may, for example, hire a professional management company to carry out its policies, operate the property on a day-to-day basis, mail notices to members, enforce rules and covenants in accordance with board policy, create and administer an annual budget, and collect assessments to maintain the property.

Although the bookkeeping and assessment collection tasks could be delegated to that management company, the association's treasurer still would be responsible for oversight of the finances and for ensuring that the manager appropriately implemented related policies. The same principle is true for any operational authority given to the board by state statutes, Articles of Incorporation, CC&Rs, and bylaws.

Community association boards benefit by retaining and empowering a professional management company through a well-constructed management agreement and adopting a governance model that recognizes and takes advantage of the expertise and experience of this most valuable consultant and adviser. With such expertise by their side, board members can make the best possible decisions. Together they can improve the association continually by providing the best possible customer service while protecting property values and improving the quality of life.

Adopting a policy governance model empowers a community association management company to carry out the day-to-day operations of a community. Enlightened boards of directors who support this arrangement are more likely to limit their activities to oversight and policy making and to avoid micromanaging.

Just as the governing documents and management practices have evolved over decades, so have governance models.

Many boards realize that their role is one of oversight rather than of day-to-day operation of the community. They realize or may have learned the hard way that when unpaid volunteers are expected to work too hard, especially at duties best left to professionals, the result often is board burnout. What's more, when unrealistic time requirements and difficult activities are expected, it becomes increasingly difficult to find volunteers to govern a community association. The solution is to adopt a standard model that allows the board to hire a manager to implement its policies and directives and to strive to meet its goals. Doing so would preclude micromanaging and promote efficiency and accountability.

This model limits the time a board needs to spend operating the community. It creates a professional system of oversight while empowering managers to act in their highest capacities as advisers and skilled practitioners of community and property management. The California Association of Community Managers is promoting such a model to its members with reportedly stunning results. It is an exciting development that promises a bright future for community association boards, members, and managers.

The benefits seem clear, and while this change in philosophy and operation may take a few years to become dominant, it seems inevitable that eventually it will replace the labor-intensive standard operational model used by boards and managers since the beginning of the industry. It presents an opportunity to establish consistency, cost effectiveness, and professionalism for a better community experience by the members.

If the mantra is to "maintain, protect, and enhance the value of the assets," what better way to realize it? What could be more beneficial than converting boards into strategic policy-making bodies and allowing trained, skilled management professionals to operate associations on a day-to-day basis within the parameters of those policies and strategic initiatives?

These seem to be simple expectations to fulfill. History indicates, however, that sometimes it is easy to lose sight of operating the association from a professional perspective as the multimillion-dollar not-for-profit corporation that it is. The pathway to improving boards of directors is as clear as it is important and challenging.

IMPROVING COMMUNITY
ASSOCIATION BOARD MEETINGS

Community association board meetings are the means through which board members come together to review progress toward the strategic goals and objectives they established and to make effective decisions that positively will impact the value of the community's assets in accordance with the business judgment rule. Regardless of their ability, boards often are judged by the way they conduct their meetings. Their first step toward self-improvement in this important arena is to raise their consciousness about the impact of their public behavior as a group and to increase their sensitivity and responsiveness to members who monitor them. This may sound easier said than done, but some easy, specific recommendations follow.

If board members are serious about improving their meetings, the most important decision they can make is to meet only when necessary. Some meet out of habit, rather than need. Because most decisions regarding well-run associations can be made at fewer meetings, all boards should consider meetings on a bimonthly or quarterly basis, rather than monthly. If emergency business arises between meetings, it can be handled during special meetings. Most, if not all, states and governing documents authorize this course of action.

Holding fewer meetings is likely to heighten their productivity, as will embracing standards such as starting on time, adopting timed agendas, not digressing from the agenda, ensuring appropriate interaction, and adjourning on time. Adopting these practices will enable board members to improve their meetings.

Another area of improvement pertains to preparation, conduct, roles and expectations, and follow-up.

Preparation involves board members' receiving and reviewing the agenda and all supporting reports from five to seven days before the meeting. This timesaving practice allows them to ask questions about materials before the meeting. It also gives managers time to research answers and solutions, to seek legal advice, to be better prepared, and to minimize or preclude controversy.

A board of directors that took action without such proper preparation learned its lesson the hard way. After interpreting a CC&R provision that prohibited farm animals in the community, the board issued a "cease and desist" letter to a homeowner whose pet was a Vietnamese pot-bellied pig. The irate homeowner arrived at a board meeting with a television crew and his beloved pig in tow.

With the camera rolling, the homeowner demanded that the board rescind its decision. The heated exchange that ensued was aired nationally on the late night news. After seeking legal counsel, the board reconsidered its decision. The pig stayed.

Had the board researched the issue and secured legal advice before taking action, this embarrassing situation and the ridicule that followed would have been avoided. This experience serves not only as a lesson learned but also as a perfect example of the importance of professional advisers in properly conducting the affairs of a community.

Preparation also includes making certain that the meeting room arrangements are appropriate for the conduct of a professional meeting. Meeting table, chairs, lighting, room temperature, water, audio-visual placement, and even place cards should be arranged before board members arrive. It is important to remember that the board meeting is not a theatrical performance for members in attendance. It is a working meeting of the board of directors of a multimillion-dollar not-for-profit corporation. Homeowners typically may address the board regarding topics of interest or concern to them during an open forum held immediately preceding the call to order. In Hawaii, however, homeowners may be allowed to speak throughout the meeting.

Conduct of the meeting should be orderly, focused, and friendly. Adopting simple parliamentary rules and procedures can help ensure that necessary information is exchanged and decisions made in a positive, professional manner. The most common parliamentary procedures are based on one of eleven editions of *Robert's Rules of Order*. Although numerous publications include "Robert's Rules" in their titles, the only official, current version is the eleventh edition of *Robert's Rules of Order Newly Revised* published by Da Capo Press.

Revised approximately every ten years, the most current edition automatically supersedes all previous editions for all organizations whose bylaws establish a parliamentary authority that includes "Robert's Rules" in its title. The next revision is expected in 2020 or 2021.

A community association's board president or presiding officer doesn't need to be a parliamentarian to apply these simple rules. Simplified and condensed versions of them are available from the

National Association of Parliamentarians' website, at bookstores, and other online sources.

"Friendly formality" is an excellent standard for board-presiding officers and meeting participants. Behaving in a friendly yet formal manner helps maintain a tone of civility and professionalism as the board conducts its business.

Board members and managers who understand and accept their roles and mutual expectations at meetings are more likely to make better decisions that benefit homeowners. Their roles and responsibilities should be adopted and updated periodically, and their procedures should facilitate their productivity and success.

Meeting these goals is more likely if boards adopt timed agendas and schedule meetings at times that allow board members to be home by dinner. Doing so would resolve the major causes of board burnout: too many long meetings that are dominated by those who deter productivity and that adjourn too late. Most important, it would improve board meetings significantly and minimize burnout.

IMPROVING MEASUREMENTS OF COMMUNITY ASSOCIATION SUCCESS

In the future every board and manager will need to be keenly aware of the association's viability in the market or face practical and market obsolescence. The needs of yesterday's members will not be the same as tomorrow's. Association leadership and management must evolve to maintain viability in an ever-competitive market environment. How will they do this? How will boards be able to know what their priorities should be?

One way for boards to measure success will be to create a baseline for the value metric. In a real estate market where values are trending downward, for example, if the subject association's values are trending down at the same rate as comparable properties, a case might be made that the board is doing an adequate job of maintaining value. If the value is trending down but more slowly than comparable properties, then the board probably is doing a good job of maintaining value. If values are falling faster than comparable properties, then the board is failing dramatically. If, however, the association's values are rising in a downward market, then the board deserves a standing ovation!

This information needs to form the kernel of every communication with the members. Homeowners need to be shown how to measure the success of the association, its board, and its manager. In the future, boards will need to recite and emphasize the fundamental reason for the covenants and rules.

All too often in the past, board and management success have been measured by a lack of complaints rather than by the value of the assets. This "lack of complaints" yardstick may, in fact, be measuring lack of interest or a weak connection between the community and its members, rather than satisfaction with the board, management, or community in general.

Members are not self-motivated by this system. They are at best complacent and at worst resentful of the board for being able to levy assessments and enforce CC&Rs and rules they had no voice in creating and, frankly, can't see the need for because they fail to connect them with the protection of their home's value. Future boards must focus on issues that matter to members, and chief among them should be the value of their homes.

Every newsletter and personal communication needs to be written with a "value of the asset" perspective in mind. Rules and covenants exist to protect the values, and it is just that simple. You can't dry your towels over the balcony railings because they are unsightly to others, especially to prospective home buyers visiting the property. The same applies to every covenant and rule.

These raise some obvious questions: How do boards know what the values are at any given time? How do they establish baseline values?

Baseline values can be established anytime. An association can select two or three units and have an appraiser do a valuation of them annually or every two years. This method eliminates any risk of basing values on sales prices that are subject to the vagaries of seller and buyer motivation that may have an emotional basis and not be connected to the true appraised value of the property.

These are simple concepts that should be applied to every association now and in the future. Future boards will need to grasp them if the community association market is to remain healthy. Their doing so is important to measuring the success and continued improvement of community associations.

CONCLUSION

Community associations will continue to flourish, especially if they improve the performance of their boards of directors, the productivity of their meetings, and their measurements of success.

The community association process is complicated. When association members interact honestly, openly, and productively, they are more likely to collaborate successfully for their mutual benefit and to strengthen their emotional equity in their associations. Improving boards of directors and their meetings is essential to that success.

It is true that tension and conflict are inevitable, but it is also true that they can be resolved. Effective board members who are committed to high standards of excellence and reasonableness are critical in this regard.

DAVID AND SANDRA
appreciate the board's outreach efforts

Myth: Board members prefer meeting in near solitude to well-attended meetings.

Buster: Board members publicize board and annual meetings effectively to enhance attendance.

David and Sandra realized the importance of the board's outreach efforts and their using every possible means to publicize association meetings. As their family got busier with work responsibilities and their children's school and sports activities, Sandra decided not to run for reelection to their association's board of directors. The community seemed to be working the same as always; no news was good news.

Then one day on her way home she saw a yard sign posted for the annual homeowners meeting that same night. Apparently members would vote on adopting a special assessment. Why had she not been made aware of this? As soon as she got home, she checked the community website, and, sure enough, there was the meeting notice with links to the assessment description.

Wow. She was out of touch and worried that if she hadn't read the notice, maybe others hadn't either. As a former board member, she knew how much work went into these meetings and how important it was for association members to understand and support the need for a special assessment. Accordingly, she emailed a few neighbors and was delighted to know that all of them were aware of the meeting and its purpose. Apparently she was the only one in the dark.

Next, she checked the mail pile. There, in the middle of what she thought was junk mail, was the meeting notification with a voting proxy form. Most interesting, the envelope was opened—David had read it. She called his cell, and, sure enough, he planned to attend and assumed that she would. Apparently she was the only one in the dark.

The board's outreach efforts had been successful: The community manager had publicized the meeting in every possible way, including the usual postings on bulletin boards and at the website, yard signs, emails, and snail mail. Ironically, the most old-fashioned medium, the yard sign, was the one that got Sandra's attention.

FREQUENTLY ASKED QUESTIONS

Q1: What regular information can homeowners expect to receive from their boards of directors?

A1: Homeowners should receive regular updates from their boards of directors via newsletters, email, websites, and other forms of communication embraced by its association. Subjects should include the financial performance of the association, planned projects, committee activities, calendar of events, etc.

Q2: What is the best way for a homeowner to communicate with a community manager about an upcoming board or annual meeting?

A2: Although homeowners should feel free to ask their community managers about meetings via telephone, in writing, or in person, the best way is via email. This is likely to shorten response time while creating a documented trail for all parties to follow.

Q3: What is the proper attire for board members, community managers, and homeowners to wear at board and annual meetings?

A3: Business or business casual is the best attire for board or annual meetings.

Q4: What are the consequences of a board of directors not meeting its fiduciary duty to homeowners, and what constitutes a breach of that duty?

A4: A board of directors can face serious consequences for failing to meet its fiduciary responsibilities. Board members can breach their responsibility in numerous ways. These include profiting personally because of a decision, showing favoritism, and retaliating against someone who disagrees with the board's decisions. Any time board members do not act in good faith, they can be held personally liable for both monetary and punitive damages and will find that their directors' and officers' insurance does not cover them for those bad actions.

Q5: How can homeowners measure the success of their board of directors and of their community managers?

A5: There are numerous ways to measure a board of directors' success. One of the primary ways is the increase in value of homes within the community. Additionally, improvement in financial performance, reduction in delinquencies, and an increase in community participation are strong indicators of a strong, successful board of directors.

CHAPTER 6

How to Improve Community Associations by Adapting to External Forces

There are two big forces at work, external and internal. We have
very little control over external forces . . . What really matters is the
internal force. How do I respond? Over that I have complete control.

—LEO F. BUSCAGLIA
American professor, motivational speaker

INTRODUCTION

The spectacular growth of community associations in the United States and beyond is the result of adapting to needs, meeting demands, resolving issues, and forecasting the future.

As the needs, interests, expectations, and demands of homeowners have changed, so have community associations. Economies of scale have allowed developers and builders to offer a wide variety of amenity packages that attract targeted buyers. Boards of directors have relied increasingly on management companies to excel in protecting property values while building community spirit.

Indeed, looking backward brings to mind remarkable growth, lessons learned, and hope for the future. Looking forward, however, brings to mind the necessity to consider how community associations must adapt to external forces over which they have no control. Their successful adaptation is essential to improving community associations. Consistent with Leo F. Buscaglia's query, how will community associations respond in the future to external forces such as the priorities of developers, changes in technology and media, and the effects of legislation? Those challenges will be examined in this chapter, as will their impact on improving community associations.

ADAPTING DEVELOPERS' GOALS TO MEET DEMAND

Any discussion about improving community associations must recognize that developers are absolutely critical to their continued success and improvement. Since the development of the first American condominium association, Greystone Manor, in Salt Lake City, Utah, in 1960, the development industry has come a long way.

It also has learned important lessons along the way. They range from raising their construction standards to exercising leadership in areas such as initial budgets, professional expertise, boards of directors, ongoing training, green communities, and industry advocacy. From these lessons learned they will be able to build a better foundation from which to define new goals and meet evolving demands.

Lessons learned

Critics of community associations often focus on problems and issues that occurred early in their history. While much of the criticism was justified at the time, the good news is that the industry and homeowners benefited from lessons learned by developers. This was especially true for the quality of homes and board governance of associations.

Early challenges to the industry, for example, entailed a significant number of construction defect lawsuits and, in many cases, poor planning for community association infrastructure and amenities. The extent of shoddy construction in the late 1990s resulted in a cottage industry for law firms that specialized in this arena.

Some construction was so sloppy that entire buildings had to be replaced. One community association in the Southwest, for example, experienced an unbelievable number of issues, beginning with water intrusion through literally all the windows in the community. Several of its buildings sank into the ground because they were constructed over a "borrow pit" (a place where earth is borrowed to use elsewhere) in which the replaced soil had not been compacted properly. Its homes that were bought by members collapsed because the studs in their walls were 24 inches apart, rather than the 16 inches required by the Uniform Building Code. Drainage throughout the property was so poor that rain and irrigation water drained into homes and carports. Perhaps most incredible, the community association's swimming pool popped out of the ground due to exceedingly high underground water pressure.

Because the builder refused to assist in any way, the community association had no alternative other than to file a lawsuit. Not surprisingly, a sympathetic jury awarded the plaintiffs sufficient funds to make the necessary repairs and replacements.

Although this was an extreme case, during that period many other community associations experienced similar issues with a similar lack of empathy from their developers. Hindsight indicates that these problems developed as inexperienced developers tried to meet the high demand for community association housing.

Poor architectural designs, untrained laborers, and the lack of quality supervision, coupled in many cases with inferior building materials, resulted in catastrophes like the one mentioned above. To make the situation worse, city and county building inspectors were constrained by a lack of education, experience, and time to provide adequate inspections at their job sites.

More recently, however, condominium owners in a southern association were surprised to receive notes that their building's foundation was being reinforced at no cost to them. Apparently a resident complained that the building was sinking, and the association responded. No special assessments were announced, and no new ones were considered. Relying on its reserve fund, the association even offered free hotel lodging to residents if the water and utilities were turned off for a significant period. Although no one enjoyed the necessary inconveniences associated with that kind of repair, homeowners were delighted that they were made. What a difference in customer service!

Akin to the construction defect problem in community associations were infrastructure shortcomings: recreation areas not large enough to accommodate the community's residents; trees and shrubs planted over sewer and water lines; inadequate parking for residents and guests; underpowered pumps and motors for gates and swimming pool filtration systems; inadequate compacting in and around refuse facilities, causing costly asphalt failure; etc. Dealing with these problems often resulted in boards of directors having no alternative other than to enact significant assessment increases and/or special assessments.

Frustrated with costly litigation and tarnished reputations, the development industry has improved by leaps and bounds in terms of construction quality and infrastructure in the twenty-first century. This does not mean that challenges do not persist. It does mean, however, that buyers are much more likely to find their dream homes in community associations today than they were in the latter part of the twentieth century.

The best developers today embrace their role in making those dreams a reality. Opportunities for improving their products remain abundant. A good place to start would be for the industry to become more involved with organizations that provide professional services to community associations. On the other hand, perhaps it is time for owner-affiliated organizations such as the CAI to become more involved with the development industry. The development industry provided the seed money for CAI, but, unfortunately, withdrew as a participant.

Developers also learned the hard way that governing documents should be easy to read and to understand. Accordingly, in addition to improving their housing products and increasing their industry participation in educational development, they should focus anew on CC&Rs, bylaws, rules, and regulations.

These important documents should be written so that typical homeowners can understand them without legal advice. The developers' attorneys who draft initial governing documents need to be charged with this responsibility. By doing so they will preclude countless problems and promote peace and harmony in the future— provided, of course, that homeowners read them.

Governing documents should focus on structural or governance issues, avoid trendy topics, and offer appropriate flexibility. If CC&Rs, which are difficult to amend, include specific, timely items such as bans on solar panels, they will be outdated soon. They may reflect the values of the era in which they were adopted, but community values change. Homeowners who eschewed solar panels twenty years earlier might now demand them. What's more, yesterday's restrictions in today's CC&Rs could result in stereotypical news stories about an association being anti-solar or anti-environment.

Empowering the board in the governing documents to adopt specific rules or requiring a vote periodically to affirm existing CC&Rs would add needed flexibility to the rule-making process and increase homeowner satisfaction.

Although the task will be challenging, it will be easier to develop initial reader-friendly documents for consideration by a community association's first board of directors than it will be to improve them later.

Today's developers are much more forward thinking, partly because of these and other lessons learned. Simply meeting the demand for housing is not good enough. Their goals must be adapted, rather, to meet the demand for high-quality homes that are wise investments in community associations with appropriate amenities.

Reputable automobile manufacturers witness the return of satisfied customers, so, too, can reputable developers of community associations.

Initial budgets

Developers can improve community associations by exercising effective leadership early in the development process. Their initiating and ensuring sound budgeting practices that reflect realistic and predictable expenses, for example, will result in fewer traumas for community associations as they mature. They need to pay careful attention that their initial budget for an association includes an adequate schedule of anticipated future capital replacements.

Today's community associations typically set aside reserves for capital expenditures and replacement of capital items as needed. If hallway carpeting in a condominium building is rated to last ten years, for example, then a developer might create a capital replacement reserve budget that includes funds to replace it. The association should set aside a fixed amount each year toward the anticipated cost of that replacement.

Many potential buyers of homes in community associations are encouraged to give special attention to the capital reserve study and whether it is funded. A thorough and complete reserve budget that is funded helps eliminate assessment surprises and the need for special assessments for property upkeep or equipment replacement. It also can add value for many buyers.

By developing a sound, appropriately encompassing initial reserve budget, developers can help community associations start on the right track. They can include items that often are forgotten, such as the life cycle of vegetation, plumbing, and electrical. Because replacing trees, shrubs, grass, etc., within the first ten years of a community association's life often results in considerable non-budgeted expenditures, costs should be included in either the operating or reserve section of a budget.

Although these assets may have long lives, including them as a line item in the budget alerts community association leaders that in time these assets will need to be maintained and/or replaced.

On a related note, a periodic operating expense line item should be included to inspect all common area plumbing for root intrusion and toiletries that could cause blockage. Unfortunately, blockage of sewer lines often results in grave consequences such as flooring and ceiling damage or, even worse, mold. Even today, mold damage to units remains one of the main sources for litigation in community associations. Preventive maintenance would resolve this issue.

The need to budget for preventative maintenance of a community association's assets is paramount. Timely maintenance of common area assets, for example, will not only help forestall and prevent unnecessary special assessments or assessment increases but also increase the life expectancy of these assets. This, in turn, will have a favorable impact on reserve allocations.

Professional expertise

From the conception of their communities, developers also should have the proper professionals in place to serve their communities. They should, for example, hire a reputable management company, an attorney with experience dealing with community associations, a certified public accountant with knowledge of generally accepted accounting practices pertaining to community associations, a community association–specific insurance agent, a reserve specialist, a landscape maintenance firm with experience dealing with community associations of the size being developed, etc. Having these experts in place when the first homeowner moves in will pay dividends to the developer and to the community association.

Boards of directors

Scheduling periodic board of director meetings as soon as practical is another important consideration. The timing of the first board and membership meetings is articulated in a community association's bylaws and/or CC&Rs. These documents typically allow the developer to have more of its employees than homeowners on the board of directors until a specified number of homes are sold. The wisest developers allow homeowners on the board as soon as possible. Doing so would be a positive gesture on the part of the developer and would provide for a good training ground for future elected home-owner board members.

Bimonthly or quarterly board meetings that commence no later than four-thirty p.m. with thirty-minute open forums for homeowner input are appropriate. Following one-hour timed meeting agendas would get the community association off on the right foot in terms of how to conduct its business pragmatically.

A proper first board of directors meeting agenda should include electing officers and establishing committees that are specified in the CC&Rs or bylaws.

While the governing documents may specify committees such as an Architectural Review Committee, the board may appoint others. These can be as varied as a welcoming or a maintenance committee. What-ever their focus, these committees should have specific charges, time lines, and directives to report their advice to their boards of directors.

Ongoing training

Perhaps the most important key to success for community associa-tions is ongoing training. The first session should be held before the first board meeting and should target board members, homeown-ers, and the developer's employees. Defining and reinforcing mutual expectations and responsibilities during these sessions are an invest-ment in future peace and harmony.

The management firm retained for the association should be pre-pared to provide this initial and ongoing training for the targeted groups.

Follow-up orientations for new homeowners are very important. Clearly, the orientation provided for new homeowners often is as cursory as it is insufficient. Sales agents have little time other than to give the unit owners their governing documents and homeowner pamphlets without explaining the details.

Complicating this is the fact that at the time of purchase most new owners are more focused on other challenges, such as having their furniture moved, getting their children situated in a new school, coordinating the installation of their utilities and cable or satellite television, etc. Not enough time is available to concentrate on understanding the CC&Rs, bylaws, rules and regulations, and architectural requirements (for planned communities)—all of which are critical documents for all new homeowners to understand. Complete documentation in the form of a new homeowner's orientation binder, useful information on the association's website, and frequent orientations for new homeowners can address this challenge.

Relationships

Nothing ensures the success of a new community like frequent, complete communication about the association/manager/developer relationship. It is important to keep in mind that the relationship between the developer and the buyer is a "buyer/seller" relationship.

Many people believe that buyer/seller relationships are inherently adversarial, with one party intent on selling something for the highest profit possible and the other party equally intent on buying it for the lowest cost possible. Given this premise, it should be no surprise that careful, complete, and continual communication is required to build and maintain healthy productive relationships between the developer and association members. A clear understanding of each other's roles is required to create harmony and success for the community.

The developer serves various roles in the new community, often including that of developer, builder, homeowner, and board member. The interest of the developer and builder is to create an asset that can be marketed and sold for the maximum profit possible. In other words, the goal is to establish the highest value possible for the assets.

The concurrent role of developers as board members and

association members is exactly the same: to create the highest possible value for the units in the most economical way. In other words, they want to accomplish exactly the same goals that the nondeveloper members are or soon will be trying to accomplish.

In modern community associations this is a common practice and leads to a responsive, transparent relationship among all parties. The trust and commonality established in these early stages of an association's life eliminates conflict and lays a strong foundation for leadership and management that will carry the community successfully far into the future.

Green communities

The community association model is uniquely adaptable to meet the growing need for greener living. CC&Rs and rules can offer incentives for green initiatives, and association activities often focus on conservation and other environmental issues.

As developers adapt their goals to meet evolving demands, they also are focusing on their community associations' infrastructure. They realize that "green communities" simply make sense because they are not only environmentally friendly but also cost-effective. This means community associations can spend less on utilities and, in many cases, maintenance. Depending on their geographic locations, they significantly can reduce costs for electricity and/or gas by investing in solar heating for pools and clubhouses.

Landscape that requires minimal irrigation is becoming much more prevalent in community associations throughout the United States, especially in the southwest where rain and access to water are at a premium. Municipalities such as Las Vegas, for example, are giving developers little choice but to develop community associations that utilize little or no water in their common areas.

Where watering is required, it often is done via drip irrigation systems controlled by ground moisture sensing devices tied to irrigation controllers. Other water conservation efforts over the years have caused developers to install low-flow toilets and shower heads in community association homes and common facilities.

Most developers are adapting their goals by incorporating these important "green" policies in construction and landscaping. More are expected to join their ranks, either voluntarily or out of necessity. Their actions will help them meet consumer demands for more environmentally friendly homes and gardens.

In these areas and more, developers will continue to adapt their goals to meet demands of community association members. Above all, they will bear in mind the priorities of protecting property values while developing a sense of community.

ADAPTING TO CHANGES IN TECHNOLOGY

The role of technology in the community association industry, as in all industries, is ever-changing. Adapting to technology changes requires community associations and management firms to adopt a reactive or proactive strategy to continue to serve their client base and provide for expected needs and wants. How do you differentiate the two? Playing catch-up as technology evolves and others experiment with it is reactive. Embracing innovation and shaping customers' expectations are proactive. For community associations, both strategies can be useful at different times and in different ways.

Plans and strategies for using the latest technology to benefit association members must be consistent with state laws, especially as they pertain to meetings and related issues such as notices, participation, and voting.

Reacting and shaping

Both reacting and shaping involve dealing with factors regarding transparency and visibility of data, taking the social electronic community to the actual community, and matching community association technology with other similar service industries such as banking or utilities.

As the community association industry continues to evolve, it will be important for associations and the companies who manage them to understand when to shape technology and when to react. The role technology plays should reduce processing times from weeks to days, days to hours, hours to minutes, and eventually minutes to seconds. Service delivery via the electronic medium must improve and continue to replace inefficient human services.

The industry today is somewhat reactive as it tries to catch up with the expectations of homeowners. Service providers ranging from pizza delivery and banking to Amazon.com and eBay cause their customers to expect the same standards from other providers.

Many homeowners, for example, utilize online banking and other services that employ much more progressive technology than current community associations. To remain competitive, management companies will need to adopt the same technology and information standards as the most advanced industries. Above all, they must strive to meet homeowners' expectations of 24/7 access to information exchanges in real time.

Increasingly, homeowners expect access to information at the same level and speed provided by other industries. Many also thrive in a paperless environment and prefer to read documents online, rather than as hard copies. Community associations and management firms throughout the country are taking giant steps in that direction.

Shaping homeowners' expectations can help create emotional equity via technology. Management firms and associations can play an integral role in using technology in innovative, cost-effective, and efficient ways that most homeowners probably never imagined, much less expected. In setting new standards and shaping new expectations they can learn from the examples of cutting-edge leaders like Apple, Google, and PayPal. In effect, these technological giants created a need where none existed. They will need to be proactive in "pushing" information to homeowners, rather than simply posting information or links to information on association websites.

The key will be balancing reactive development with shaping home buyers' and homeowners' expectations. Management companies need to move quickly to catch up but even more quickly to help set the stage for the next revolution in technology.

Transparency

The Information Age has ushered in expectations for instant access to information and data. Community associations are not exempt. Their information must be "pushed out" and delivered. Their financials, violations, CC&Rs, management action plans, and a wide variety of reports and announcements should be available on demand, 24/7.

Homeowners and board members alike want immediate access to data when they want it and how they want it. They also expect the same high standards of consistency, accuracy, and completeness met by other industries that employ electronic media.

Board meetings

Board members and managers can employ a rich variety of technology tools to promote homeowners' participation. Although some of them may believe that a quiet meeting with no homeowners in attendance may be a "best" meeting, homeowners should be welcomed and encouraged to attend.

A best practice for increasing participation and improving accessibility and transparency, however, is to make board meetings and information easily accessible through technology. Allowing meetings to be presented via products such as Skype, GoToMeeting, or WebEx would allow homeowners to monitor them from their homes. It is exceedingly easy to provide links to access meetings online or through archives and relatively easy to host websites at which written board materials are posted in real time.

This technology also facilitates remote attendance at board meetings by board members, committee members, community managers, and other professionals to the benefit of the entire community.

Many large associations already broadcast their meetings via closed-circuit television. The government of Dubai went so far as to stipulate in its community association statute the right of boards of directors to conduct their meetings online. While most states have not addressed this technology in their statutes, it seems certain to become an important trend nationwide and even worldwide as boards of directors realize they can meet effectively without having to go to a central meeting place.

By trailblazing effective meeting procedures and the use of technology, boards can continue to improve their associations. They also can select from a wide array of technological advancements that benefit and inform homeowners. Examples include posting meeting minutes and financial statements on community association websites; paying assessments online; and submitting work orders, inquiries, and other requests via the Internet.

Peace of mind

Technological advances in security add to the peace of mind of homeowners in many communities. Community associations were among the first to provide security-enhancement equipment such as entry gates that recognize license plates of homeowners and guests, digital cameras that provide clear and comprehensive visual coverage of all common areas, and eye and face recognition for entry into homeowner units and common areas.

Based on their success, associations are likely to continue to be early innovators, including by using the Internet efficiently and effectively to enhance peace of mind. Websites that offer resale disclosure information and detailed information about all other facets of a community association's operations aid homeowners, boards of directors, and community management. Such transparency promotes confidence among members and enhances their comfort levels.

The end of the path for improving community associations deals with peace, harmony, security, and the resultant maintenance or enhancement of property values. Advancements in technology have and will continue to play significant roles in reaching that ideal. Board members and managers should be at the forefront of adapting to these advancements and to employ them to improve community associations.

ADAPTING TO CHANGES
IN THE MEDIA LANDSCAPE

The biggest change in the media landscape for management companies and community associations is that traditional media are no longer linchpins to their medium or communication strategy.

Historically, if an organization wanted to disseminate information about itself, it would send a news release to television, radio, and newspaper reporters either directly or via a syndicated news service wire. In either case, audiences depended on the reporter and his or her editors to receive the release and to decide whether the information was worth producing and publishing.

With only minutes, sometimes seconds, to be included in local and national news, stories inevitably landed on the editing room floor. Consumers largely had access only to what the media decided was important or had time and space to report.

Depending on this gatekeeping system was not necessarily bad. After all, the media was tagged the "fourth branch of government" largely because of investigative journalism. Dedicated to reporting the truth while objectively (sometimes mercilessly) unveiling a story, investigative journalists held high-profile people and institutions accountable to the public.

What has changed about this process is the result of the decrease in the number of practicing journalists.

In 2011 the Federal Communications Commission released an exhaustive study, *The Information Needs of Communities*. Its statistics confirm what our intuition and behavior have told us for years.

The numbers are staggering but not surprising. Some of the most interesting are listed below:

> The number of television network news personnel declined by half since the late 1980s.

> The number of daily newspaper personnel shrank by more than 25 percent since 2006. Some major newspapers reduced their staffs by half during the same period.

> Approximately as many Americans subscribe to newspapers today as did in 1945. The number of households, however, is three times larger.

> The number of all-news local radio stations dropped from fifty in the mid-1980s to thirty. Cumulatively, they reach a third of the country.

Why the paradigm shift? The digital age has carved a path for consumers to be their own journalists. The Internet and its myriad of push-and-pull communication media have given consumers the ability to customize their own news.

Why would consumers wait for a morning newspaper to be delivered when they can "Google it" or read Twitter feeds via smart phones immediately upon waking-up? Why would they watch the news at given times when their favorite reporters or social media managers tweet all day about the latest developments in the same news stories? Why would they watch an entire program when they can see the same news video clips and more via YouTube?

These are only three examples of the dozens of social media, and new ones emerge daily. Alongside these, consider the thousands of blogs, micro blogs, and review sites that do much more than offer a medium for consumers to post photographs, videos, comments, etc., or to re-tweet.

Consumer-driven blogs make available platforms for people to own, write, and design their own online "papers" that push unfiltered news at any time. Review sites like Yelp and City Search give consumers a place to offer opinions and to share information freely or to editorialize with arguably very little monitoring. In this online world, editors and fact-checkers are a rarity, and consumers can share and connect directly with one another.

Why does this changing landscape affect community associations, and why should they adapt? Essentially, community associations have two primary audiences to consider, namely, home buyers and homeowners, and one major goal for each, namely, to protect and elevate their community's reputation. Through digital media, they can reach both audiences simultaneously for relatively little cost.

Simply stated, there is no cheaper, faster way to accomplish this communication, and an increasing number of technologically savvy persons demand it. The trend is irreversible, and it impacts community associations and virtually every other service industry. If for no other reason, that ability justifies their embracing and adapting to these powerful new tools.

Why should community associations use social media to reach home buyers and homeowners? Reasons abound, but the main ones are fairly obvious: To begin with, house hunting almost always begins online, and home buyers are likely to access social media while searching for potential homes and neighborhoods. The same social media can benefit homeowners, especially because their emotional equity and connection to neighbors will evolve when information is available readily and exchanged easily.

Accordingly, community associations should offer online content that tells their neighborhood's story. A community website, for example, can highlight members of the board of directors, provide photographs and descriptions of amenities, post activity calendars, and, with permission from residents, display photograph and video galleries of community socials. By doing so they help home buyers understand the community they are considering and help homeowners stay connected with their neighbors.

Websites are only the beginning. If a board member or other homeowner is willing to manage it, a community Facebook page can be very helpful in sharing community news updates, invitations to meetings, and recaps of events. These pages are increasingly popular, allowing connections not only among neighbors but also with other community management companies that have Facebook pages.

Social media also facilitates communication between management companies and the homeowners they serve. Although they traditionally communicate through the board of directors, when both are connected via a social medium, anyone can garner any information offered. Homeowners and home buyers can discover a management company's promotions, programs, and tips, while management companies can gain insight into their thoughts and needs. Such streamlined interaction can be mutually beneficial in countless ways.

One noteworthy benefit of social media accessibility is improved customer service. When a couple in a mid-Atlantic region association experienced a power outage at their home, for example, they used a mobile phone to post the news on their community and management company's Facebook page.

Within minutes the company's social media monitor responded by confirming that it was a group outage and that the power company had been called. The homeowners felt relieved to know that the problem was being addressed and that they were not alone.

Emergencies typically are reported by calling the proper authorities, but, in this case, communicating via social media expedited the response and resulted in exemplary customer service.

Monitoring review sites and creating and maintaining blogs are time-consuming, but automatic alerts that are generated by new postings can save time. Volunteers who have the time to handle this responsibility usually enjoy it immensely and are appreciated just as much.

How will community associations respond to the changing media landscape? Actually, they already are—and will continue to do so.

For their part, management companies already are connecting with their homeowners and potential home buyers. Some of their blogs share expertise about association living. They offer great resources to homeowners and boards not only for administrative tips but also for seasonal tips for home and lawn care, and even general tips about living better in and around the home. These blogs are especially appreciated and productive when they provide areas for homeowners to post comments, share insights, or direct questions to association experts.

Ways to use social media to advantage are boundless. One industry leader recently suggested, for example, that management companies develop smart phone apps specifically for targeted associations. Another suggested that the industry focus not on the current media but, rather, on identifying its technology-related needs that can be met by future digital media. This is appropriate, especially because tools that weren't imagined ten years ago are prevalent today—and their rate of evolution is likely to accelerate.

Websites, social channels, blogs, micro blogs, and numerous other online media are new technological cornerstones of the industry. They ensure that community associations and management companies are connecting with each other and with home buyers, ultimately protecting and elevating their reputations and building emotional equity among their neighbors.

Community associations will continue to adapt to the changing media landscape while utilizing its new tools to improve not only their sales and retention but also their customer service. Their keys to success require staying at the forefront of using technology to do a better job. Impressively, they are doing just that.

ADAPTING TO CHANGES IN LEGISLATION

Adapting to legislative changes does not mean simply reacting to the actions of elected bodies at the local, state, and federal levels. It means getting involved early in the process and staying involved at all stages. By mustering their internal forces to impact legislation, community associations can avoid being surprised by new laws that are imposed upon them without their prior knowledge or participation.

One of the many lessons I have learned during my years in public service is that in the legislative process, if you are not at the table, you are on the menu. This is particularly true for community associations.

When issues arise affecting community associations, there are no shortages of "experts" offering advice, especially regarding legislation. In most cases critics are readily available to offer a host of solutions in search of problems.

Critics deserve to be heard, but their proposals must be examined and evaluated wisely, thoroughly, and fairly. Equally important, conflicting viewpoints must be considered just as respectfully. Above all, fair and responsible public discourse and transparency can promote productive collaboration among stakeholders.

Just as a healthy community association requires the participation of its members, protecting the viability of associations requires their engagement in the legislative arena. Their failure to engage in the process could be detrimental to their continued success. What's more, their ability to respond swiftly, appropriately, and effectively to the legislative proposals offered by activists is as important, if not more so, than initiating laws and adapting to them after they are enacted.

Critics of community associations sometimes act as if associations were a new and alien concept to the American housing scene. They often levy charges that associations are out-of-control petty dictatorships or unconstitutional governments.

While there are some legitimate criticisms of community associations, these are not among them. Community associations are the embodiment of American values. In fact, the concept of community governance goes back to the founding of our country.

Think back to the pilgrims who founded what became the Massachusetts Colony. Headed to Virginia to make a new life for themselves, they got lost, fell behind schedule, and landed many miles from their destination in late fall, with little time to prepare for the impending winter.

Before disembarking from the Mayflower, the colonists sat down and mapped out the rules by which they would govern their community in a new and strange land. Their document, the Mayflower Compact, was an influential factor in shaping the Massachusetts Constitution and, later, the United States Constitution.

Clearly, the concept of a community association through which neighbors make agreements among themselves regarding how to order their affairs is a fundamental American concept.

With such a rich history woven into the fabric of community associations, one would think that they would be celebrated as embodiments of the American ideals. Of course, anyone who thought that would be wrong.

For a variety of reasons, community associations face a barrage of legislative proposals that threaten their viability. These challenges generally come in two broad areas: The first comprises stand-alone bills that target specific rules for community associations. The second set of challenges targets the basic governance structure of community associations.

These proposed laws usually are inspired by association critics or by sensational news stories about problems within a specific association. Many of them are overreaching, ignoring community associations' structure of democratic self-governance that embodies the essence of local control typically espoused by conservatives.

Why should homeowners care about these proposals? The common ownership element of each community association means that its homeowners either will succeed together or sink together when faced with the threat of overzealous regulation. The belief that the least state or federal government intervention is the best outcome should be the basis for their greater involvement. If for no other reason, their participation should be motivated by the impact of statutes on their property values.

Property in a community association has a price premium of from at least 5 to 6 percent*, according to the American Enterprise Institute. This premium largely is attributed to the common amenities and to rules that govern the aesthetics in an association.

Preserving and enhancing association property values requires an environment in which informed board members may make decisions about rules and their enforcement. If that process is undermined by legislative micromanaging or a negligent board, the vitality of the community is threatened. It is through this lens that the need for associations to either adapt to an activist legislative environment or adapt the environment to their own needs is understood.

The most easily understood set of challenges community associations face comprises legislative efforts to override association rules. At first blush such issues seem minor, perhaps petty, but the collective effect undermines neighborhood governance and property values.

Various surveys indicate clearly that homeowners support rules that protect the aesthetics of their community associations. Almost 80 percent of them specifically support community rules that protect and enhance their property values, according to a Zogby industry survey.

Interestingly, however, support for those rules crumbles when the rule is applied to an issue that either is the subject of a popular trend or is near and dear to the heart of an individual. In such cases, rather than seeking to change rules through their community's governing process, affected homeowners go to the press or the legislature to override the community preferences in question.

An explosion of so-called "Right to" legislation has impacted

---

* *Do Homeowners Associations Raise Property Values? What are Private Governments Worth?*, Amanda Agan, Alexander Tabarrok, Regulation, Fall 2005, p. 17.

community associations during the last ten years. Such efforts sought to override community-adopted rules by prohibiting associations from governing certain activities within their boundaries. Solar panels, clotheslines, xeriscaping, gardening, displaying the American and foreign flags, granting rights to nonresidents to enter secure property, satellite dishes, and ham radio antennas are among the subjects of legislation to strip associations of their rights to regulate such matters.

Considered individually, such bills seem minor, but, cumulatively, they would have a two-fold cumulative effect:

First, they would condition homeowners to act outside the scope of their neighborhood governance process. If they object to rules, they should urge their elected boards to change them, typically by majority vote.

An association's governing documents define the process and votes required to change not only rules and regulations but even bylaws. Some changes require adoption by the membership, rather than only by the board. Realistically, this process should be simpler, less time-consuming, and perhaps even less expensive than lobbying a state legislature or U.S. Congress to take action.

Such a path helps ensure that proponents of change within a community garner broad bases of support as they build a majority consensus on the board. As the elected representatives of the community, board members are in the best position to determine what rules fit the values and preferences of the community. Working through that democratic process to build consensus is a key to building emotional equity in a strong community.

The second cumulative effect of these efforts is that second-guessing by remote legislative bodies undermines these civic virtues. As more and more topics are removed from the purview of the board, the ability of the association to maintain the value of the properties diminishes.

Owning property in a community association imposes rights and obligations that are very modern in their conceptualization. Association members contractually agree to legal obligations to pay assessments and to obey the rules adopted by the community's elected board.

Often disputes that reflect a lack of knowledge about homeowners' obligations trigger legislative proposals that affect the governance structure of community associations. These are more problematic than the so-called "Right to" proposals because they target key governance mechanisms needed to maintain an association's common ownership portions. What's more, they often seek to impose upon all associations in a state the changes sought by homeowners from one association.

Legislators must understand the most basic concepts: A community association is a form of governance, not a government. Most community associations are nonprofit corporations that operate for the mutual benefit of their members. Their powers are defined not only in statutes but also in their respective CC&Rs, bylaws, and rules that are overseen by their boards.

Courts treat the legal relationships between the association and its members as private contractual relationships. This means that the association's powers are limited by its governing documents and changeable by its members, either through direct votes or by board action. By engaging in neighborhood governance and entering into agreements with their neighbors, homeowners in an association are exercising their sovereign rights under the U.S. Constitution. The failure to understand this relationship as one of private contract rather than one of government often is a source of friction for homeowners, boards, and legislatures.

Legislative challenges to the governance or operational structure of community associations will determine the future viability of the community association model. Since the historic housing crash of 2008, there has been a divergence related to proposed state and federal regulatory changes impacting community associations. Addressing these issues will be key to ensuring the marketability of homes in community associations for the next generation of buyers.

In response to the housing crisis, federal agencies have undertaken a massive overhaul of mortgage regulations. The rules for who gets a mortgage, for what type of property, in what type of community, are in the midst of a radical overhaul.

One issue that recently was interjected into this process is requiring underwriters to examine the finances not only of the borrower, but also of the community association in which a home will be bought. The Federal Housing Administration (FHA), for example, has emerged as the de facto underwriter for many condominium mortgages. This agency emphasizes assessment delinquency rates to the extent that it will not issue a mortgage in a condominium association in which more than 15 percent of the units are sixty days delinquent in their assessments.

In response to these policies and to ensure that home buyers can obtain mortgages, many associations intensified their enforcement of assessment obligations. Their efforts triggered a backlash from state legislators after reports about associations foreclosing on properties for past due assessments and about perceived abuses by collection agents.

The result is a set of state laws that conflict with emerging federal mortgage standards. While the FHA requires, for example, that no more than 15 percent of units in an association be sixty days late in assessments, North Carolina law prohibits associations from taking any actions against delinquent homeowners until they are at least ninety days past due. While the law in North Carolina clearly is designed to protect some delinquent homeowners in community associations, its conflict with evolving mortgage regulations may hurt all members of those communities.

Because disputes within community associations are considered private contractual disputes, many homeowners feel powerless when they find themselves in conflict with the association leadership. While the vast majority of associations are well run and managed, there are outliers hampered by lack of member involvement or by board members who do not understand their roles. Their uninformed decisions can result in truly horrific stories.

Resolving private contractual disputes typically requires obtaining counsel and pursuing the matter through the courts. This is costly and inefficient. Homeowners and boards need greater access to tools that facilitate more efficient conflict resolution through alternative means. This may include board education, community-based alternative dispute resolution mechanisms, or pro bono forums through which members or boards can resolve conflicts.

State-sponsored ombudsperson programs have been a siren song for policy makers for some time. The concept is that a state-appointed ombudsperson could facilitate dispute resolution on behalf of homeowners in community associations. Three states—Nevada, Virginia, and Florida—have ombudsperson programs, and Colorado has established an association information office.

Such programs remove dispute resolution from the community and move it to a centralized location, typically the state capital. This actually complicates resolving the dispute because the process becomes more formal and expensive.

These programs also suffer from their lack of mutuality: The government appointees are authorized only to side with homeowners against boards. They cannot work with elected boards to deal with rogue homeowners who ignore assessment obligations or break rules repeatedly.

The private contractual nature of the relationship between the homeowner and community further complicates the process because ombudspersons generally are not legal parties to the dispute and have limited abilities to intervene.

The results of these programs have been mixed, at best. A review of complaints filed with Nevada's ombudsperson indicated that most of them were baseless.

Community associations are democratic organizations that affect the lives of millions of homeowners in the United States and beyond. In any democratic system, there is room for issues to arise. Such issues are inherent in any system that relies on volunteers and the participation of members.

Too often the legislative focus on community associations is misplaced by assuming the structure of community associations is the catalyst for conflict. As a result, legislative remedies amount to a legislature substituting its judgment for the will of the community as the solution. They should focus instead on providing mechanisms to encourage homeowners' participation in the governance process and the educational tools needed to build consensus, govern effectively, and resolve conflict.

The key for associations to adapt to a period of greater government scrutiny and regulation is to set a positive agenda for community associations that empowers homeowners and not government. To ensure the long-term viability of community associations, such an agenda should include mechanisms for accomplishing the following:

> Establish incentives to ensure educated and vibrant boards.

> Educate consumers about their rights and responsibilities in community associations.

> Ensure that consumers understand the value of qualified community management.

> Promote transparency and disclosure to consumers at time of sale with a right of rescission.

> Provide a clear legal framework that clearly outlines the roles and responsibilities of stakeholders in a community association.

> Engage legislators about the value of community associations and the need to respect their internal democratic processes.

In the current legislative environment, it is more critical than ever that community associations adapt to changing laws governing their communities as well as to the reality that protecting the viability of their community requires engagement in both its governance and policy matters. Communities are more likely to thrive if they stay abreast of changing legal requirements and speak out to ensure that policy makers can make informed decisions. Those who neglect their governance issues and do not stay on top of changing requirements may very well find themselves in a situation of permanent decline and reduced access to mortgage financing.

The stakes are high. Fortunately, these negative outcomes are avoidable, and their positive alternatives are achievable. Engagement in the governance and legislative process by homeowners is the key to ensuring the future vibrancy of their communities.

CONCLUSION

Looking backward enables an analysis of the growth of community associations and an evaluation of the lessons learned along the way. These lessons serve as the foundation from which to make significant improvements, particularly as associations respond to external forces, including developers, changes in technology and media, and legislation.

Developers clearly are in unique positions to create community associations with a strong base that includes high-quality construction and infrastructure, sound initial budgets that reflect realistic and predictable expenses, suitable professional expertise, and smooth beginnings and transitions for boards of directors. They also should provide ongoing training and establish clear lines of communication that promote strong relationships with association members. Equally important, they can respond to the public's demand for more green communities.

Improving community associations will depend to a large extent on their ability to adapt to changes in technology and media. By reacting to technology changes and shaping expectations for better, faster service, they can promote transparency and improve customer service. By using social media to enhance interaction and strengthen relationships, they can help homeowners build emotional equity in communities.

Equally important, community associations must engage more effectively in the legislative arena. Instead of simply adapting to changes, they must get involved in shaping those changes. Their priorities must include ensuring public discourse and transparency as legislation is considered. Such engagement is beneficial in protecting not only the basic governance structure of community associations but also property values.

The growth of community associations has been phenomenal, but their future looks even better, largely because of their commitment to improve. By mustering their internal forces to learn from the past in improving the future, they can adapt most effectively and successfully to external forces.

DAVID AND SANDRA
use social media to their advantage

Myth: Social media technology is used for fun and has no legitimate value in connecting homeowners, their board, and the community management company.

Buster: Many homeowners use social media technologies to spread news quickly and to solve issues.

David and Sandra often rely on social media to communicate effectively within the association. One day, for example, Sandra loaded her car and headed to the clubhouse pool with her daughter.

Swim season was starting, and the young mother had been busy helping to plan the association's Summer Party and opening weekend of the pool. While her family didn't use the pool frequently, the party was always a fun way for the neighborhood kids to let off some steam and celebrate the school year's end.

As Sandra was parking, she realized she hadn't received her new pool card and had no way to enter the area to begin setting up. How frustrating. Because it was a Saturday, the management company was closed, so she couldn't call the manager.

Before resorting to climbing the fence, she called David at home. He immediately logged on to their management company's Facebook page and posted the issue. Within minutes, an employee posted a response that his colleague who lived nearby could deliver Sandra's new card to her at the pool.

Sandra was actually surprised and relieved this avenue worked. Thanks to social media, she connected with the management company almost immediately, completed the arrangements timely, and the party was a huge success.

FREQUENTLY ASKED QUESTIONS

Q1: When does a developer's responsibility to a community association end?

A1: The point at which a developer's responsibility to a community association ends varies by state and by association. Specific information should be available from your association manager or board of directors. Alternatively, you can search the Internet or seek legal counsel.

Generally, however, developers are required to serve on an association's board of directors for a period specified in its CC&Rs and/ or bylaws.

They also have specific responsibilities related to the maintenance and warranty guarantees for the assets, buildings, and infrastructure they built within the community association. The details regarding how long developers will be required for those guarantees will be defined in the appropriate warranty documents and, in many cases, in related state statutes.

A manufacturer, for example, might guarantee an entry gate motor for a year. If the motor fails to operate that long and its manufacturer goes out of business, the developer is responsible for replacing it.

Roof work is also typically guaranteed by contractors for one year. If, however, they fail within ten years because of shoddy workmanship and/or materials, many state statutes require developers to replace them.

Q2: I just bought a home in a new community association. How soon can I expect a membership meeting to be scheduled, and how can I be appointed to the board of directors?

A2: Your community association's CC&Rs dictate when the first membership meeting shall take place. Your bylaws will explain the procedures for nominating yourself and/or other homeowners for possible election to the board of directors.

Electing volunteer homeowners to serve on the board usually is the most important item of the first and successive annual association membership meetings. The CC&Rs usually allow the board of directors to comprise more members during the community association's initial development stages.

Board members decide when and how often to have meetings. Some meet monthly, bimonthly, or quarterly, but the best practice is to meet when there is necessary business to conduct.

Q3: My association board of directors is conducting online meetings, but I don't own a computer. How can I access the meetings?

A3: If you don't own a computer you can access online meetings via smart phones or tablets. Alternatively, you can use public computers at public libraries and Internet cafes. Another option is to request that a speaker telephone with a conference line be utilized so that you can at least listen to the meeting.

Q4: What blogs and websites provide good content and tips about association living?

A4: Some of the best blogs and websites about association living are listed below:

> `Association Times: http://www.associationtimes.com
> HOA Management Blog: http://www.hoamanagement-blog.com/
> Condo Association Management Blog: http://www.condo-association.com/blog/

> HOA Management Directory Blog:
  http://www.hoamanagementdirectory.com/blog.html
> Condo and HOA Law Blog:
  http://CondoandHOALawBlog.com

Q5: How can homeowners keep up with the many changes in state laws?

A5: Preserving your investment in your community association requires participating in its governance and being aware of changing laws at the local, state, and federal levels.

First and foremost, the community manager should keep the board and homeowners informed about legislative issues that may affect community operations or governance.

Second, the board or homeowners can join local or national trade groups dedicated to providing information about changing laws for community associations.

Finally, the board should build relationships with key county, state, and federal elected officials by inviting them to community meetings or social events. Building personal relationships with key legislators helps to ensure that you can call on them when needed to discuss a key proposal.

Timely information also is available readily from your local chamber of commerce, your local chapter of the CAI, or your association's and other websites.

Many state legislatures host great online resources. Texas's website, for example, allows stakeholders to register for alerts about legislative action related to selected issues, to search specific topics, and to track bills of interest. Some of the major state sites are listed below:

> Arizona: http://www.azleg.gov/
> California: http://www.legislature.ca.gov/
> Florida: http://www.myfloridahouse.gov/
> Texas: http://www.capitol.state.tx.us/

PART III

FORECASTING COMMUNITY ASSOCIATIONS

CHAPTER 7

Why the Community Association Phenomenon Will Grow Worldwide

Never doubt that a small group of thoughtful, committed citizens
can change the world. Indeed, it is the only thing that ever has.

—MARGARET MEAD
American cultural anthropologist

INTRODUCTION

As the community association concept and industry have matured
and evolved, the current model has created a firestorm of approval
and acceptance in the United States and beyond. Its success is based
on the almost universal appeal of living in communities governed by
volunteer boards and with neighbors who share a common interest.
That appeal is based not only on mutual benefit but also on demand
for infrastructure and amenities created and maintained at levels
selected by the members through their boards of directors.

Add to that the ability of the members to enhance or change
those standards by participating in the community association, and
the result is a model that establishes an immediacy of governance not
found in other corporations or community governance models. In
some countries that is an entirely new concept.

By volunteering for committees, running for the board, and electing
leaders, members can exercise the ultimate in democratic prerogatives.
As Margaret Mead would have understood all too well, cumulatively,

small groups of volunteers are changing the style and standard of living throughout the world through community associations.

Indeed, many countries are experiencing an explosion in the development of community associations. In the United States our northern and southern neighbors, Canada and Mexico, can attest to this. In places like Dubai and Queensland, Australia, literally all new residential development involves a community association. Large-scale planned community development is the norm in South Africa as well. In the corridor from Sao Paulo, Brazil, through Buenos Aires, Argentina, ending in Santiago, Chile, 8 percent of all residential growth involves community associations.

The phenomenon that has become so popular in the United States is being perfected elsewhere. The best entry access technology, for example, is coming from Dubai. Witness the Dubai Pearl, a mixed-use community association that championed face recognition technology for homeowner entry into their homes and common areas. The Burj Khalifa, another mixed-use community association in Dubai, currently is the tallest building in the world. Interestingly, while many large-scale community associations in the United States include churches, many in the Middle East include mosques.

Although their operations, structures, and concepts are similar to those in the United States, community associations have different names around the world: "Strata property," "body corporate," "commonhold," and "timeshare," for example, are terms used to describe the ownership structure and governing bodies in other countries. They are explored in detail throughout this chapter, which also addresses the worldwide trends and growth of community associations and their counterparts. More specifically, it focuses on the equivalence of community associations in Canada, Mexico, South America, Europe, the Middle East, Asia, South Africa, and Australia.

These regions differ dramatically, but they often are compared. In 2010, for example, *Newsweek* ranked "The World's Best Countries." Its comparison was based on five categories of national well-being:

economic competitiveness, education, health, political environment, and quality of life. The result was a list of one hundred nations that ranked Finland first and included Canada, 7; United States, 11; Singapore, 20; Chile, 30; Costa Rica, 35; United Arab Emirates, 43; Mexico, 45; Brazil, 48; and South Africa, 82. Their success certainly is conducive to the growth of community associations that is examined herein.

UNDERSTANDING CANADA'S CONDOMINIUM COMMUNITIES

The community association lifestyle in Canada dates back to 1967, when the country's first condominium was developed in Edmonton, Alberta, and its first high-rise condominium was built in Nepean, Ontario. Today there are condominiums in many parts of the country, although, as in the rest of the world, their highest concentration is in metropolitan areas.

Just as state governments in the United States pass laws that govern the operation of their respective community associations, so, too, do Canada's provinces. Their related terminology also may vary by province. In British Columbia, for example, community associations are referred to as "strata." The term also is used in South Africa and in other regions that modeled their governing documents on principles from the first strata laws created in Australia in 1961.

Like community associations in the United States, strata can be residential, commercial, industrial, and other types of buildings. Also like them, they generally are a form of ownership in which members own their units and a share of the common area.

In Québec they are referred to as syndicates of co-ownership, while in Ontario, by comparison, they are referred to as condominiums and are governed by the Condominium Act of 1998. In that province each development establishes a corporation to manage the daily maintenance and operations.

Regardless of the terminology used in creating these legal structures, it is their lifestyle and immense market appeal that are evident in their growth. In 2005, for example, during the height of the global economy, 17,000 new housing units were sold in these developments in Toronto, Ontario—more than anywhere in the world. Trailing distantly was the second most popular location, Miami, Florida, where 7,500 units were sold in community associations.

The formation of trade and interest groups in Canada exceeds the model in the United States: As the popularity of community associations became apparent, it spawned national and regional organizations that enthusiastically support both developers and managers of condominium developments.

The Canadian Condominium Institute (CCI) has sixteen chapters across the country, from Vancouver to Nova Scotia. A multidisciplinary organization, it offers membership to condominium corporations, professionals, sponsors, and members. According to its website, CCI is the only national association to serve as a clearinghouse and research center on condominium issues and activities across the country. It also lobbies provincial and federal governments to improve legislation.

The Association of Condominium Managers of Ontario was formed in 1977 to represent the collective aims of condominium managers and management companies. It offers continuing education and the Registered Condominium Manager designation. The Association of Condominium Managers of Alberta was formed in 1997 and serves professional managers in the province by advancing best practices and education. It also offers advanced designations for experienced managers who meet their education requirements.

This strong level of professional support and the related market demand for community living are evidence that the United States' neighbors to the north strongly embrace community associations.

EXPLORING TIMESHARE
VACATION RESORTS IN MEXICO

The three largest metropolitan centers in Mexico are Guadalajara, Monterrey, and its capital, Mexico City. Due to a growing middle class and relatively stable economy, these areas have embraced the community association model in the form of high-rise condominiums and gated communities. In addition, developers have filled the coastline with timeshare resorts that attract investors from the United States, Canada, and beyond.

A timeshare in Mexico may be the perfect lifestyle purchase for anyone who dreams of owning an affordable vacation home on a beach that can be enjoyed year-round. It is an opportunity to "buy time," typically in one-week increments, at the resort of choice. In effect, a timeshare is a long-term vacation lease that can offer many attractive lifestyle amenities.

Spawned in Europe in 1960, this type of ownership has evolved in other countries and throughout the United States since 1974. The result is a worldwide market of vacation properties. They generally include a percentage "fee simple ownership" in the property and the creation of a community association to collect maintenance fees, manage the property, and provide the resort amenities.

Timeshare properties are available in many vacation destinations. In Mexico they offer a foreign purchaser an opportunity to own real estate, an option that was not available only a few years ago. Today 16 percent of timeshare communities worldwide are in South America, 40 percent of which are in Mexico.

This is possible because the federal government responded to the concerns of outside investors. Foreign ownership of real property in Mexico was prohibited until 1993. At that time the laws were changed to provide stability and protection by creating a real estate trust. This may have made no difference to timeshare developers who were Mexican citizens, but those who were United States or foreign corporations wanted this protection for their investments.

A timeshare purchase gives the buyer the right to use the property (generally not a specific unit) at the time agreed in the purchase agreement. In exchange the owner pays a purchase price (a one-time cost, unless financed), plus an annual maintenance fee. Required regardless of whether the time purchased is used, the annual maintenance fee is similar to an annual assessment or maintenance fee in a traditional community association.

In these resort settings the maintenance fees typically cover all of the vacation resort hotel's amenities. These include maid service, bars and restaurants, recreation centers, transportation, replacement of furniture and fixtures (as specified in the reserve component study), social activities, and additional luxuries like spas and golf courses.

One of the primary differences between a community association formed to manage a timeshare community and its traditional counterpart is the control maintained by the developer or resort manager. For resorts such as Starwood, Wyndham, Accor, Hyatt, Hilton, Marriott, or Disney to maintain stable operations, their developers build strong controls into their governing documents. Provisions may, for example, allow them to elect the boards of directors and maintain operational controls for an extended period—perhaps from twenty-five to fifty years. This means that if the maintenance fees are not limited by contracts, operators can pass on cost increases to the members.

One of the benefits of timeshare ownership is the ability to trade or exchange the use of a property for another location. This is done through global organizations established to create a marketplace for timeshare owners. RCI and Interval International, for example, created and maintain a marketplace for timeshare sale and exchange.

From Baja to Cancún, timeshares have opened the door to vacation property ownership for those who live within or beyond the Mexican borders. They offer the community association lifestyle and benefits to all who appreciate it at home and want to enjoy it during their travels abroad.

DISCOVERING DEVELOPMENTS
IN SOUTH AMERICA

Community associations are thriving throughout South America, including in Brazil, Buenos Aires, Chile, and Costa Rica. Their popularity indicates that they will continue to grow and diversify to meet lifestyle and economic preferences. The need for this type of high-density, affordable housing reflects the limited space and dense populations of many South American urban areas.

With a population of more than 192 million, for example, Brazil is the fifth largest country in the world. Because approximately 84 percent of its population is concentrated in its urban areas, high-density, multiresidential housing is needed. Community associations in the form of condominium communities serve this need and also provide opportunities for foreign investment in desirable beach communities.

In Buenos Aires, the capital of Argentina, condominiums are as prevalent as in many other urban environments. These condos are popular with local owners as well as with foreign investors from North America, Western Europe, Russia, and Brazil. Although pricing reflects a stable real estate market, sales volume currently is low. Property often is priced in American dollars, and currency fluctuations tend to keep buyers on the sidelines.

Another form of ownership that is new to Buenos Aires is the condo hotel, which is a condominium with hotel-like amenities and services. Each condo is owned by a single owner (as opposed to a timeshare), and the owner can choose to live on-site or to turn it over to the hotel and rent it permanently or part time.

With economic and population growth, apartments, condominiums, and cooperatives are an important part of the housing mix in the more densely populated areas of Chile. Referred to as "co-ownership," this type of housing was authorized and defined in the Chilean Real Estate Co-Ownership Act of 1997. That law also clarified the obligations of co-owners, addressed insurance requirements, and established a guide for managing community associations.

Costa Rica, with its beautiful beachfront property, is home to many condominium and town home communities. According to the World Fact Book, an online resource published by the Central Intelligence Agency, this small country continues to experience political stability and relatively high education levels. As a result, it continues to attract one of the highest rates of foreign investment in South America. This condition creates a robust real estate market for local as well as foreign investors and future retirees.

Community associations in Costa Rica offer a wide range of amenities and lifestyle choices to serve this expanding market. As in other countries, specific laws were adopted to govern these communities.

In 1999, for example, the Regulatory Law of Condominium Properties authorized the use of horizontal, vertical, and mixed-use buildings; defined owners' rights and obligations; and established rules for condominium assembly and management.

Clearly, in these and other regions throughout South America, community associations offer the lifestyle choices and pricing options that appeal to growing populations of the regions.

TOURING COMMUNITY ASSOCIATIONS IN EUROPE

Multiunit housing in the form of apartments or flats has been common for centuries in many parts of Europe. Often they are either large residences that were subdivided by floors or even larger buildings that operate like the stock cooperatives defined in Chapter 1. In Europe they are more commonly referred to as housing cooperatives or co-ops.

As in a typical American cooperative, buyers in a European housing cooperative own a share of stock in the corporation that owns the entire property, including its living units, building interiors and exteriors, and land. A purchaser buys stock in the cooperative, and that stock ownership provides the owner the right to occupy a particular unit under the terms of a proprietary lease. The co-op maintains the exterior and interior of the building, including the grounds but not the interior of the units. The cooperative, through its board, also has some authority to approve the stock purchaser.

While stock cooperatives are a popular form of housing in Europe, some European countries also employ a form of ownership consistent with the condominium structure used widely in the United States.

In England and Wales "condominium" is synonymous with "commonhold," a term introduced in the Commonhold and Leasehold Reform Act of 2002. Commonholds remain a small part of the housing market in that region, however. Only ninety-seven units in twelve developments existed in 2009.

In Denmark 5 percent of homes are referred to as "owner apartments" that are bought and sold in the same manner as single-family homes. Their structure is similar to a community association's: Buyers create a homeowners association through a joint ownership agreement, and they divide the cost of maintaining the joint property based on their share of ownership.

Condominiums were introduced formally in Norway in 1983. In 2012 approximately 19 percent of Norwegian homes were condominiums, almost mirroring the 20 percent who live in community associations in the United States.

Despite this growth in Norway, community association living is sparse throughout Europe. The reasons are as diverse as the European countries and reflect the historical housing trends of those areas. France, for example, has an oversupply of social housing, and Portugal has a history of excessive bureaucracy relating to housing.

Looking toward the future, housing development will depend on the speed of the financial recovery. Since the recession, residential construction has fallen sharply across Europe. An upward shift would require significantly greater access to mortgage credit.

ANALYZING THE CONDOMINIUM
BOOM IN THE MIDDLE EAST

Dubai, an "emirate" or political territory ruled by a dynastic Muslim monarch in the United Arab Emirates (UAE), is home to the world's tallest building: The Burj Khalifa is 2,716.5 feet and 160 stories high. With residential and commercial condominiums, plus a five-star luxury hotel, it also is the world's tallest community association.

Residences include nine hundred studio and one-, two-, and three-bedroom suites with amenities such as acres of open green spaces, tennis courts, water features, four-story health and recreation annex, library, cigar club, and gourmet market. Advertising for the Burj Khalifa targets buyers who desire an exclusive address and a lifestyle that includes a wide range of high-end amenities.

Businesses also can experience the prestige of this address by purchasing commercial condominiums called "corporate suites." The entrance lobby to the thirty-seven stories of corporate suites features an express elevator to the sky lobby, valet parking, and built-in state-of-the-art technology and security.

Last, but not least, the Armani Hotel features one hundred and sixty guest suites, eight restaurants, shopping, florist, and bakery. This unique property has been created and ultimately will be governed consistent with the community association model.

Although the Burj is the most recognizable building in Dubai, this iconic landmark is only one of hundreds of buildings constructed since 2002, and virtually all of them are community associations. The construction boom was fueled by the government's decision to transition from an oil-based to a service- and tourism-based economy.

This transition created a business hub for information technology and finance, attracting companies from throughout the world. As a result, Dubai is home to a very diverse population. As of 2005 only 17 percent of its population comprised UAE nationals, with 83 percent coming from other countries, primarily India and Pakistan.

In 2006 the Real Estate Regulatory Agency (RERA) authorized

foreigners to purchase real estate in Dubai. Today the ownership in condominiums mirrors the country's diversity and includes Americans, Europeans, Russians, and Asians who purchased a condominium in Dubai as their first, second, or even third home.

As for community associations in the United States, education is the key to creating informed and engaged home buyers, homeowners, and board members. The added population and market demand for the community association lifestyle in Dubai created a new industry that recognized the need to educate and train the professionals who will support these communities.

In 2007 the Dubai Real Estate Institute (DREI) was created, becoming the Middle East's first academic institute in real estate education. In 2008 it partnered with RERA to deliver certified training for real estate professionals in Dubai.

In 2011 the second Middle East Association Managers Conference was held. RERA and DREI sanctioned the event to bring together professional managers and consultants who worked with condominium representatives during a two-day program that included participating in educational activities and sharing best practices. They turned to the United States for help, and CAI accepted their invitation to take a delegation of leading professionals to share their expertise.

Many common challenges were discussed, including the impact of a housing decline that began in 2008 and the resulting foreclosures and assessment collection issues faced by community associations. This problem is exacerbated in Dubai, due to a lack of understanding the responsibilities of condominium ownership, the percentage of part-time absentee owners, and newly enacted laws.

This collaboration was so successful that it continues today. CAI awarded the first Professional Community Association Manager (PCAM) designations to community managers in Dubai in May, 2012.

Community associations in Dubai are structured based on governing documents similar to those used in the United States. A declaration, for example, creates an entity known as an owners association (OA), and its community rules are the equivalent of American CC&Rs.

In 2007 the Government of Dubai issued Law 27, which is titled, "Concerning Ownership of Jointly Owned Properties in Dubai." Each OA must have its own constitution that contains the language referenced in this law, defines key terms, and establishes requirements for governance. It includes many of the provisions included in the bylaws of American community associations.

Community managers in Dubai often are under contract with or in the employ of an association's developers, rather than being employed directly by the association. Even so, they have day-to-day responsibilities that are very similar to those of managers who work directly for community associations: They maintain the common areas; prepare for and attend board meetings; and work to resolve conflict, while educating owners about the rules adopted for the common good.

This is not an unheard-of arrangement in the United States. A large-scale community association near Sacramento, California, for example, has been managed under that arrangement for more than twenty years and has garnered numerous awards for excellence from CAI and other organizations. The manager of the property has not changed in the entire history of the project and has provided continuity and consistency that is valued by the members and the developer.

Construction of high-rise buildings continues in Dubai, and the professional management of community associations will continue to evolve as more and more owners become educated and involved in the governance of their communities. Following Dubai's example, Abu Dhabi, Qatar, and Saudi Arabia also are embracing the developments that reflect the community association lifestyle and operating principles.

COMPARING OWNERSHIP OPTIONS IN ASIA

In densely populated parts of Asia, high-rise and multifamily residential communities are a common necessity.

In Singapore most of the housing comprises condominiums and "flats" built and maintained by the governmental Housing Development Board. The term "condo" generally refers to housing that has added lifestyle or luxury components such as security guards and recreational amenities.

Hong Kong is one of the most densely populated areas in the world. Thirty-six of the world's one hundred tallest residential buildings are in this city, with 95 percent of them inhabited by ethnic Chinese and 5 percent by other groups. More people in Hong Kong live or work above the fourteenth floor than anywhere else on the globe, making it the world's most vertical city.

In addition to high-rise living, Hong Kong is home to many high-end luxury communities. The Beverly Hills is an exclusive luxury development whose amenities include a shared Ferretti 550 Italian Super Yacht, limousine service, and a 350-meter indoor car-racing track.

With more than 23 million residents, Shanghai is now the largest city in the world. It has grown dramatically since 1990 and, like Hong Kong and Singapore, includes many multiresidential buildings.

One of the most consistent similarities among these jewels of Asia is the density of their populations. This dynamic creates the necessity of living in vertical structures, which results in the creation of higher density housing.

The structure and management of these communities appears to be similar to operations in the United States. In Hong Kong, for example, the document that creates ownership interests and governs cost allocation is called the Deed of Mutual Covenant. This document also defines maintenance responsibilities and shared expenses such as internal partition walls and utility connections.

In Singapore, managers, sometimes called property officers, are hired to attend meetings, take minutes, manage complaints, and coordinate repairs and maintenance. Their duties are similar to those of their counterparts in the United States.

REVEALING HOUSING
TRENDS IN SOUTH AFRICA

Clearly, community association development is serving the needs of many homeowners throughout the world. That also is the case in South Africa, where strata is the common form of ownership in multiresidential communities.

The term "strata" originally referred to a multilevel building with horizontal boundaries on different levels or strata. Another common term, "sectional title," referred to the section of title owned by the buyer. In South Africa today, strata or sectional title is a form of ownership and governance that is used to refer to primarily single-family home communities that commonly are called "estates."

In 1986 South Africa adopted its Sectional Title Act governing estate communities. It defines the rights of owners and creates the governing requirements. In addition, the Company Act, which is similar to the Corporations Code in the United States, defines the business requirements of companies in South Africa.

The specific documents created for an estate community are based on these laws. The Articles of Association or Memorandum of Incorporation define how the board of directors is elected, prescribe how committees are appointed, and create management guidelines. Because most developments are large, gated communities and employ on-site community managers and staff, management companies are rare at this writing.

South Africa has diverse cultures and languages and a population of approximately 50 million, according to the 2010 Census. Its most populated cities are Johannesburg, Soweto, and Cape Town, followed by Durban and Pretoria. The lifestyle appeal for estate communities is based primarily on the location and demographics of the neighborhoods.

The country has a mixed economy, a high rate of poverty, and a low gross domestic product per capita. This contributes to a relatively high crime rate and motivates decisions about housing choices. Many of those living in estate communities do so because of the additional investment in security features, including controlled access and regular patrols. Other features include recreational amenities, golf courses, country clubs, and hotels.

Managers in South Africa often face infrastructure challenges that would be unimaginable in most parts of the United States. The routine delivery of electricity and water often are disrupted. When housing developments moved to the suburbs, creating housing options for a larger segment of the population, a corresponding investment was not made in electric generation and water treatment facilities. Consequently, there is not enough of either to meet demand. Living without electricity or water for two or three days is common, even in the luxury estate communities.

At a large estate community in Durban, the board recently developed electricity generation and solar panel usage policies to help homeowners and the association deal with fluctuations in the delivery of electricity. Looking ahead, they are researching methods to store electricity that can be redistributed during these major fluctuations in supply.

Until recently, managers in South Africa were isolated and had little opportunity to share best practices or work together to solve challenging problems. In 2010, however, they formed the Association of Residential Communities to support and optimize estate leadership.

They also looked internationally for educational opportunities and expert advice. The CAI partnered with them to provide educational activities and best practices for their estate managers and volunteer board members. In 2012 two South African managers earned their PCAM designations.

COMPLETING THE TOUR
WITH A LOOK AT AUSTRALIA

This chapter began with a reference to the first strata title (law), which was created in Australia in 1961. Although there are various models for structuring community associations, parts of Canada, South

Africa, Singapore, and Malaysia have adopted the Australian system as the basis for their legal structures.

Today strata communities in Australia offer a wide variety of lifestyle choices. From the high-rise beachfront condominiums in Queensland to the quiet residential enclave in Sydney, there is a desire for owners to live with others who share mutual interests.

This very popular form of home ownership has created a vibrant industry of professionals to serve them. Strata Community Australia (SCA) was formed in 1992 as the National Community Title Institute. For the past twenty years, dedicated volunteers have worked to create a national organization that would provide a forum for better communication among managers and management firms throughout the country. They are developing nationally recognized qualifications for strata managers and held their first annual conference in 2012.

"Body corporate" and "Community Title" managers in Australia focus most of their time on the executive and administrative requirements for their communities. Specifically, they are responsible for financial management, meeting preparation, planning, and communication. Outside experts often are used to provide services in all areas of facilities management.

In Melbourne, Victoria, the regional chapter of SCA publishes a quarterly newsletter to educate members about all aspects of building management and operations. In the summer 2012 issue, they included the results of a 2011 survey of strata management companies.

The results of the survey revealed two factors that have the most impact on their business performance. The first is delivering excellent client services, and the second is developing and maintaining client relationships. To achieve both, 53 percent said they would recruit new staff and invest in training and development programs.

This is good news for strata community owners throughout the region, as the industry maintains its commitment to delivering the best outcomes for its clients.

CONCLUSION

As community associations continue to thrive around the globe, their boards and professional managers will focus more intensely on protecting the value of the assets for their members. As evident from this overview of community associations as a worldwide phenomenon, a significant component of creating value is the result of maintaining quality of lifestyle and the financial health of the association. As association boards shift their focus, they will adapt and change their respective governance models. By providing proactive leadership and valuable information based on experience, professional community managers will continue to empower boards with a strong foundation from which to base policy decisions for their managers to implement.

The specific components for maintaining this quality of lifestyle will vary depending on location. The owner of a timeshare in Mexico, for example, will continue to prioritize the resort amenities of a vacation home, while the owner of a townhouse in Sydney will be more interested in the routine maintenance and replacement of the common areas. Condominium owners in Vancouver and Hong Kong, by comparison, are more likely to be concerned about the fair and consistent enforcement of rules that benefit those who live in close proximity to one another.

Clearly, while the specific priorities of each association will differ, their overriding goals will remain the same, namely, to preserve the value of the assets. To achieve this goal, professional managers, vendors, and board members will rely on quality continuing education for all involved. Industry associations like the Community Associations Institute in the Unites States and the Association of Residential Communities in South Africa will be the catalyst for keeping us connected to share best practices and distribute current information.

DAVID AND SANDRA
invest in student housing for their son—in another country

Myth: Community association living is an American phenomenon, unknown in other parts of the world.

Buster: Community associations have grown phenomenally throughout the United States and are increasingly prevalent throughout the world.

David and Sandra's family matured, and their youngest son, now a senior in college, garnered an opportunity to study in Sydney, Australia, through an international student exchange program. Intrigued by how he could benefit from the experience, the three of them took a trip to learn more about the sister college and the nearby living situation.

They found that the institution's programs were ideal to complete their son's college education and that numerous nearby condominiums also were close to some of Sydney's attractions.

Also intrigued by the possibility of owning a space in Sydney, the threesome enjoyed a day of condo hunting down under. It didn't take long to surmise that owning a condo there would provide all of the amenities they were used to in their community association back home. In fact, many of the rules and benefits to which they were accustomed seemed prevalent in Sydney.

The community association lifestyle would ease their son's transition to living in a culturally different environment. In spite of being so far from home, he would be comfortable and, with few maintenance responsibilities, could manage without them. What's more, they were only a phone call away if questions arose.

Most important, David and Sandra were confident that the condo's property value would be protected in the community association. They were glad to realize that association living was available in other countries, too. What began as a need for student housing resulted in an investment property that someday could even be a second home for them.

FREQUENTLY ASKED QUESTIONS

Q1: How do the governing documents in countries such as Canada or Mexico differ generally from those in American community associations?

A1: Although community associations are developed throughout Mexico, a standard, comprehensive legal structure has not yet been achieved. A typical condominium development is created with a document called the "condominium regime," which is similar to the CC&Rs and articles of incorporation combined. This document provides the authority for an individual to be empowered as the community's manager, with the ability to make all operation decisions.

Q2: Are there any lessons learned by community associations in other countries that could be beneficial in the United States?

A2: Definitely. Community associations in the United States should learn from the advancements in high-rise building technology coming from the Middle East, sustainability projects in South Africa, and governance models in Australia.

Q3: What major countries do not have community associations?

A3: The countries that have not embraced this structure are European, primarily France, Great Britain, and Germany. Most of the metropolitan areas were developed in those regions before the community association concept became popular in the 1960s. In addition, the prevalence of socially subsidized housing in Europe diminished the market for condominiums.

Q4: Do community associations in other countries also have automatic membership and lien-based assessments?

A4: Yes. Since most countries have based their legal structure on the strata title developed in Australia, automatic membership and a form of lien-based assessments apply.

Q5: Do United States citizens who want to purchase a property abroad need special permission from their home or destination country?

A5: United States citizens do not need special permission from their home country to purchase property abroad, but the requirements of destination countries will differ. In Dubai, for example, a homebuyer must apply for a special residence visa that allows him or her to buy "foreigner's properties" and live, but not work, there. The visa can be granted only by the government and typically is valid for three years. Conversely, in Hong Kong there are no restrictions on foreign investments.

CHAPTER 8

How Community Associations Will Adapt to Changing Demographics

All the people like us are We,

And everyone else is They,

And They live over the sea,

While We live over the way,

But—would you believe it?—They look upon We

As only a sort of They!

But if you cross over the sea,

Instead of over the way,

You may end by (think of it!) looking on We

As only a sort of They!

—RUDYARD KIPLING

English writer, poet

INTRODUCTION

The history of community associations is rich in examples of how they adapt to meet the needs and demands of their changing markets. As the population in the United States grows and changes, community associations change to serve the evolving population within regions and neighborhoods.

There are no admission requirements to reside in an association, other than an interest in the neighborhood and selection of a home, coupled with the ability to pay the cost and fees. Associations are open to every demographic group, though members of some naturally are drawn to communities that house residents with similar needs and interests.

There are two notable and occasional exceptions: co-ops and active adult communities. Perhaps the most obvious example is the active adult community, which also may have some age-related restrictions permissible under federal law.

All demographic groups, including age, however, break down into social categories. Any segment of the population, for example, can be analyzed in terms of the traditional factors of race, ethnicity, and age, as well as common sociological groupings such as education, socio-economic status, and political affiliations.

Community associations reflect the demographics of society. In adapting to evolving demographics, community association leaders reflect Rudyard Kipling's words that people whom "We" see as "They" instead see themselves as "We" and us as "They." The practice of building positive relationships based on similar needs and interests is based on a growing understanding of differences and similarities in attitudes, beliefs, and behaviors.

Such insight and sensitivity should enhance community associations' success in adapting their goals, marketing, and customer service to meet the multicultural aspects of such demographic diversity in the United States. Accordingly, this chapter focuses on how they will adapt to the changing demographics in general and to multiculturalism and diversity in particular. It begins with an overview of those changes and the related language of diversity. It also highlights the impact of multiculturalism and diversity and offers specific recommendations for dealing with them.

ANALYZING THE CHANGING POPULATION

Before community associations can adapt to the changing demographics, their leaders must understand the data. Numerous sources are available, but the most relied upon is the U.S. Census Bureau, which is charged to record, analyze, interpret, and report the nation's changing demographics every ten years.

Census data

Although estimates about the future population of the United States vary, the U.S. Census of 2010 forecasts from 422 to 458 million inhabitants by 2050. In other words, expect at least 100 million more persons by midcentury than the 320 million counted in 2010.

The population is expected to increase at least 32 percent, but the geographic boundaries will remain constant. This means a greater population density will impact housing. In planning for the future, community association developers will have to consider minimizing building footprints and maximizing vertical space usage.

Also consider that the population of today and tomorrow is different from yesterday's in many ways. It is and will be not only older but also more racially and ethnically diverse. This is exceedingly obvious in light of the 2010 Census data.

The federal agency recognizes six races and an additional broad category. These are listed below:

> White (including Hispanic)

> American Indian and Alaska Native

> Asian

> Black or African American

> Multiracial (two or more races)

> Native Hawaiian and Other Pacific Islander

> Plus "Some Other Race"

The census also identified four groups that total 97.35 percent of the population and projected their changing numbers from 2010 to 2050. These projections are listed below:

	2010	2050
Non-Hispanic Whites	64.7%	46.3%
Hispanics/Latinos (any race)	16.0%	30.2%
African Americans	12.9%	13.05%
Asian Americans	4.6%	7.8%

Table 2

Population groups other than these four may be centered in different geographic regions. Cumulatively, however, at the national level they comprise only 1.65 percent of the population, according to the U.S. Census.

The four groups that comprise 97.35 percent of the population in 2010 will change significantly by 2050:

> The dominant population, non-Hispanic Whites, dropped to less than two-thirds in 2010 and will drop to less than one-half by 2050.

> The fastest growing population, Hispanics, will almost double in size, from 16 percent in 2010 to 30.2 percent in 2050.

> The Black or African American population is expected to be stable, growing only by less than 1 percent from 12.9 in 2010 to 13.05 percent in 2050 and

> The Asian American population will almost double in size, from 4.6 percent in 2010 to 7.8 percent in 2050, but will remain a relatively small minority.

These census projections are just that . . . projections. Variables such as birth rates, intermarriage, and immigration will impact these numbers.

Diversity groupings

The Equal Employment Opportunity Commission employs seven diversity groupings that can be remembered by the acrostic, REGARDS:

> › Race
> › Ethnicity
> › Gender
> › Age
> › Religion
> › Disabilities, and
> › Sexual orientation.

Countless other categories also differentiate the population, including the following:

> › Background
> › Education
> › Employment status
> › Experience
> › Family makeup and size
> › Income or wealth
> › Geography
> › Language(s)
> › Lifestyle
> › Marital status
> › Occupation
> › Philosophy, and
> › Politics.

Elements of diversity such as these offer a framework from which to analyze, understand, and adapt to targeted populations, whether they are potential home buyers or current homeowners. Above all, the focus must be on common threads that unite residents as they develop a sense of community.

A community association manager, for example, who recognizes that homeowners in an association are members of numerous religions would be wise to plan multidenominational holiday celebrations. The spirit of the occasion should be inclusive and inviting to all, instead of exclusive and exclusionary.

Another example pertains to politics: A manager who knows that homeowners are independents and members of both major political parties would be wise to invite all candidates to a forum, rather than representatives of only one party.

Equally important, a developer who knows that a particular section of a particular city attracts mostly large, young families would be wise to plan a community association with houses and amenities that cater to their needs and interests.

Extensive data are available about the changing population. They are empowering not only to planners but also to those who govern and manage community associations.

DEFINING THE LANGUAGE OF DIVERSITY

The language of diversity includes a myriad of terms. While positive terminology includes "culture" and "tolerance," negative alternatives include "discrimination," "prejudice," and "stereotypes." There is no, nor should there be, room for these negative terms in the new American community.

Because stereotyping can be unconscious, association members and managers can promote peace and harmony by raising their consciousness about it. By developing multicultural and diversity insight and competence, they will enhance their ability to help develop positive relationships and to build emotional equity in communities.

Clearly, behavior that can be interpreted as offensive or insulting by others often is unintentional. Because such behavior usually reflects insensitivity, lack of awareness, or lack of experience with or knowledge about other cultures and diverse groups, it can be stopped.

Three terms are particularly important in this arena, namely acculturation, enculturation, and ethnocentrism. They are defined and explained below:

> *Acculturation* is the practice of adapting to and adopting the traits of another culture. Later-generation immigrants may acculturate more quickly than their first-generation family members. Children who immigrate tend to acculturate more quickly than older family members.

> *Enculturation* is the practice of remaining true to your own culture. First-generation immigrants are more likely to reflect enculturation than later-generation immigrants. Intermarriage can multiply the challenges of enculturation.

> *Ethnocentrism* is the belief that a particular culture or country is superior. This "We" versus "They" mentality can hamper a community's best interest. Reflecting only the needs, interests, and customs of the dominant culture or groups without considering the preferences of other customers can lead to disastrous internal and external community relations. Understanding the richness of multiculturalism and diversity can reduce ethnocentrism.

The language of diversity in and of itself offers insight into analyzing and understanding the changing population.

UNDERSTANDING THE IMPACT OF MULTICULTURALISM AND DIVERSITY

Changing demographics mean changing markets and clientele. This, in turn, results in different needs, interests, demands, and expectations. In this respect, understanding the impact of multiculturalism and diversity is essential for the future growth and success of community associations.

Adapting to change is critical. What if a manager realizes, for example, that the community association has an increasing number of Spanish-speaking homeowners who speak little or no English? To meet their needs, the manager has numerous alternatives:

> Arrange for the homeowners to interact with a manager who speaks Spanish.

> Develop Spanish translations of newsletters and meeting notices.

> If their numbers justify the expense and effort, ask the board for authorization to develop Spanish translations of the governing documents.

> Employ technological tools, including smart phone apps that instantly and audibly translate English into the selected language.

Whatever preferred language or other characteristic differentiates one group from another should be evaluated in light of the fact that no group is homogeneous. Every group is heterogeneous and breaks down into categories. Consider your own racial, ethnic, age, or gender group, for example. Are you the same as everyone in it? Obviously not! Neither is any other person the same as every other member of any specified group.

Clearly, generalizations typically are invalid and problematic. Stereotypes typically are ridiculous when examined in the reality-based light of day. Indeed, social demographics impact cross-cultural similarities and differences. Highly educated worldwide travelers of different racial or ethnic groups, for example, may have more in common with each other than with others in their own racial or ethnic groups. If they are multilingual and have a language in common, they will be able to communicate more effectively than otherwise.

A totally different example is offered by conservatives and liberals with disabilities who may have more in common with other like-minded persons who don't have disabilities than they do with each other.

Given examples such as these, it is easy to ask: Why do stereotypes about the members of these social categories persist? Lack of experience and knowledge. That is why consciousness awareness must be raised, and understanding must be prioritized.

Change in the population of the United States is not merely inevitable, it is rampant. If developers, board members, and managers don't know how their markets are changing, how can they deal with them—and how can they succeed? Ignoring multicultural diversity and differences can impact an association's bottom line negatively. Understanding their impact can facilitate success, especially in attracting home buyers and retaining homeowners.

DEALING WITH MULTICULTURALISM AND DIVERSITY

Ignorance is no excuse for failing to develop multicultural and diversity competence. If it exists, it must be overcome through consciousness awareness and educational programs. This means identifying and overcoming cultural barriers, learning and avoiding verbal and nonverbal cross-cultural land mines, and adapting goals to meet the needs of multicultural and diverse groups.

Cultural barriers

To succeed requires overcoming cultural barriers that typically originate from three main sources: personal and interpersonal habits, lack of exposure and experience, and organizational practices.

Personal and interpersonal habits include the lack of appropriate verbal, nonverbal, and vocal communication skills. Whether conscious or unconscious, many persons reflect preconceptions, stereotypes, and judgments in their words or actions. Some deal with prejudice and discrimination, whether expressed or experienced. Many also may exhibit stress, discomfort, or inexperience in interacting with those who are significantly different. Some barriers exist simply because of lack of exposure and experience. Interaction in diverse groups and settings often results in increased understanding and acceptance.

Organizational barriers, including insensitivity to the varying needs and interests of diverse groups, must be changed at all levels. Leadership from the top is essential if an organization such as a community association or the industry itself is to develop multicultural competence.

Barriers imposed by other sources also should be identified, and strategies for overcoming all of them should be prioritized. Interestingly, positive experiences with members of different groups often are a catalyst for overcoming barriers to enjoying multiculturalism and diversity.

Developing the sophistication needed to adapt effectively to the country's demographic changes requires educational programs that encompass the following:

> Multicultural intelligence

> Understanding opportunities

> Motivation to embrace diversity

> Insight into language, culture, and traditions

> Exposure to and experience with diverse groups

> Diversity training and

> Consciousness and sensitivity.

Research and training should go beyond generalizations about cultural and generational differences. It should focus on very specific information that empowers developers, board members, managers, and homeowners to avoid cross-cultural verbal and nonverbal land mines.

Verbal land mines

Efforts should be made to increase awareness of and sensitivity about the countless verbal land mines that should be avoided in cross-cultural communication. Some of these are highlighted below:

› Not using a person's preferred self-referent can be problematic. The only way to know terminology preferences is to listen and/or to ask. Alternatives include the following:

  ‣ African American or Black?

  ‣ Anglo, Caucasian, or White?

  ‣ Hispanic, Latino/Latina, Mexican American, Cuban American . . . ?

› Using racial/ethnic/cultural/diversity humor and slurs is (or should be) offensive, even to persons who are not members of the targeted group. Examples follow:

  ‣ Speaking Spanish to a perfectly bilingual Hispanic whose reaction likely will be, "Do you think I don't understand your English?"

  ‣ Saying, "I'm having an Alzheimer's moment!" jokingly in front of a customer whose spouse suffers from it.

  ‣ Saying, "Don't be a r*t*rd!" to a customer whose child has an intellectual disability.

› Not reflecting "friendly formality" can be perceived as disrespectful and condescending. Examples follow:

  ‣ Calling a woman who is older "young lady."

  ‣ Calling persons who are older by their first names without knowing their preferences.

  ‣ Referring to a group of women as "you guys" or "you girls."

> Not pronouncing names correctly and respectfully reflects a lack of effort. Anyone who is uncertain about a pronunciation should simply ask.

> Laughing at names, pronunciation, customs, and errors is absolutely taboo.

Listening to customers to determine their preferences is as important as being aware of and sensitive about possible cross-cultural verbal land mines. It is equally important to increase awareness of and sensitivity to the countless nonverbal land mines that must be avoided in cross-cultural communication. Some of these are highlighted below:

> Using hands the way they normally are used in the United States can cause cross-cultural gaffes.

  ‣ Persons who are left-handed may be shocked and dismayed (perhaps even hurt or insulted) to know that in some cultures and groups, the left hand is considered the "dirty hand" or the "hand of the devil." The ultimate insult to them would be for someone to use his or her left hand to give them something, to pat them on the back, or in a two-handed handshake.

  ‣ "Hidden hands," whether in pockets or under the table, may be perceived as an act of hostility in cultures in which hands should be visible at all times.

  ‣ The "crooked finger" used to indicate "come here" is perceived in other cultures as the equivalent of the middle finger; or is used to call animals, as an act of hostility among equals, or as a threatening gesture to children or insolence to adults.

> Something as simple as crossed legs, thereby showing the bottom of a foot, is insulting in some cultures.

> Even making good eye contact, initiating conversation,

touching someone on the shoulder, and offering a handshake can be problematic in some cultures, especially across gender groups.

> What Americans consider "rude noises" after a meal may be not only acceptable but expected in some cultures—and not making them could be considered insulting.

> Smelling like alcohol or a food forbidden in other cultures also can cause cross-cultural customer service *faux pas*.

Observation, "listening with the eyes," and mirroring customers' behavior are absolutely imperative in avoiding verbal cross-cultural land mines.

Action steps

No one said this would be easy, but it is doable. Mastering this insight and gaining the related experience is simply step one in the process. The next step is for community associations to plan and to execute the action steps that comprise targeting the changing market that is increasingly diverse. These steps are listed below:

> Analyze the customer base.

> Research the market and potential home buyers.

> Identify ways to reach out and to engage persons from identified cultures and demographic groups.

> Plan appropriate diversity training.

> Adapt marketing strategies.

> Develop multicultural customer service strategies—and continued training!

By taking these steps, community associations can enhance their success and reap the benefits of dealing effectively with the changing demographics.

CONCLUSION

The population of the United States in 2050 will be significantly different from today's. It will be older and more diverse in terms of traditional groupings such as race, ethnicity, gender, age, religion, and disabilities. Each of these groups also can be differentiated by social categories that include education, employment, family, languages, and socioeconomic status.

To adapt to changing demographics, community association leaders must understand the language of diversity and the impact of multiculturalism and diversity. This means overcoming cultural barriers wherever they exist and planning continuing educational programs that are essential to developers, board members, home buyers, and homeowners.

Undoubtedly, the market and its clientele are changing and will continue to change. By taking specific action steps that include analyzing customer bases, engaging in market research, and modifying marketing strategies, community association leaders are more likely to adapt successfully to changing demographics.

DAVID AND SANDRA
enjoy a unifying multicultural holiday celebration

Myth: Community associations are culturally homogeneous and ignorant about cultural and religious differences.

Buster: Most boards are at least aware of different religions, cultures, and demographics and can plan events that are fair and respectful to everyone and that encourage learning and interaction among different cultures and faiths.

David and Sandra joined homeowners in a unifying multicultural holiday celebration that was respectful to all. Their favorite month was December. It was the one time of the year that all of the neighbors participated in an association event, namely, the Winter Social and House Light Tour.

Weeks before the event, neighbors readied their homes with twinkle lights and inflatable lawn characters, the more the better. Emails, website notices, yard signs, and banners invited homeowners to participate by lighting their homes and joining their neighbors at the clubhouse for hot cocoa and an international potluck dinner, followed by horse-drawn carriage rides to see the welcoming winter lights that illuminated their homes beautifully.

Each year at least one new family worried about the possibility of celebrations that would exclude their cultural or religious traditions, particularly during this special time of the year. Their worries were baseless. The board and homeowners understood and appreciated that their community was a true melting pot. Homeowners included Caucasians, Asian Americans, Indians, African Americans, Hispanic Americans, American Indians, Middle Easterners, and others—all of whom observed a variety of religious holidays and cultural traditions.

All were welcomed to organize their special activities for everyone interested. Many, including David, Sandra, and their children, celebrated Christmas but also participated in other religious celebrations for educational purposes. The entire community came together, however, at its one delightful December celebration.

The board felt that including everyone and encouraging families to bring their favorite international dishes resulted in a unifying event that attracted high attendance. The emotional equity stemming from the event was priceless.

FREQUENTLY ASKED QUESTIONS

Q1: What is the best source for more specific information about the growing population?

A1: The best source for more specific information about the growing population is the U.S. Census Bureau, www.census.gov. It offers a rich array of data and its interpretation.

Q2: What is the difference between race and ethnicity?

A2: Race is significantly broader than ethnicity. For the discussion at hand, it is limited to the six races identified by the U.S. Census, namely White (including Hispanic), American Indian and Alaska Native, Asian, Black or African American, Multiracial (two or more races), Native Hawaiian and Other Pacific Islander, and "Some Other Race."

Ethnicity is a narrower category that indicates a common heritage, including a shared language or dialect. Mexican Americans, for example, usually are Caucasians, but many Hispanics are members of other races.

Q3: What is the difference between Hispanics and Mexican Americans?

A3: Hispanic is a significantly broader category that includes Mexican Americans. All Mexican Americans are Hispanic, but not all Hispanics are Mexican Americans. The broader term includes persons of varied descents, including Cuban, Puerto Rican, and Spanish.

Q4: What is the single most important cause of prejudice and discrimination?

A4: Ignorance and lack of exposure to members of different demographic groups. Insight comes with education and experience.

Q5: What are the consequences of community associations not adapting to demographic changes?

A5: Not adapting to demographic changes could have negative consequences for community associations. Developers, for example, would risk establishing community associations that would no longer be in demand in specific areas and failing to provide suitable choices for the changing population. Those who manage and govern associations could fail in adapting their marketing, managing, and customer service strategies, resulting in failure to gain home buyers and to retain homeowners.

CHAPTER 9

How Active Adult Communities Will Serve the Aging Population

Don't spend your energy defending yesterday. Instead, spend your
energy exploiting today and the future.

—PETER DRUCKER
Management consultant

INTRODUCTION

The inimitable growth of community associations in comparison to other types of housing often is attributed to their continuing success in meeting the changing needs and interests of potential home buyers. As those who develop, govern, and manage associations studiously prepare for the future, they must consider how to adapt to population changes.

Age is among the foremost features that differentiate societal groups within changing populations, whether in the past, present, or future. Today's population in the United States, for example, is older than it was ten or more years ago and younger than it is expected to be in ten or more.

The reason is obvious: "Baby boomers," defined by the U.S. Census as having been born between 1946 and 1964, are becoming "golden boomers." Those born in 1946 were sixty-five years old in 2011. By comparison, those born in 1964 were forty-five that year and will be sixty-five in 2031. The National Association of Area Agencies on

Aging expects one of every five Americans to be older than sixty-five by that time.

While many consider sixty-five to be full retirement age, in 1983 the U.S. Social Security Administration raised it to sixty-six for anyone born between 1943 and 1954 and to sixty-seven for anyone born after 1960. In making these changes, the U.S. Congress also provided reduced benefits for retiring earlier and enhanced benefits for those who waited. These changes in retirement ages and benefits certainly will impact the lifestyle and housing needs of Americans.

The attitude of these Americans as they age tends to be consistent with the advice espoused by Peter Drucker: They tend to spend their energy exploiting their present and future rather than defending their past. The community association industry is doing the same in planning for its future and for theirs.

Specific efforts include developing active adult communities with the amenities and governing documents that meet the needs of this growing and important segment of our population. Accordingly, this chapter focuses on how the aging population will impact community associations. Its highlights include defining the active adult communities and their residents.

DEFINING ACTIVE ADULT COMMUNITIES

"Active adult communities" is the term popularized to describe community associations for residents who are older. Because they cater to this specific age group, these communities also are known widely as "fifty-five and older communities."

Because the U.S. Fair Housing Act prohibits discriminating on the basis of age or familial status in the sale or rental of housing, developers must secure waivers. To comply, they typically require that at least one member of a household be fifty-five years of age or older. This ensures their compliance with federal regulations requiring that at least 80 percent of households include at least one member who is fifty-five years or older.

Active adult communities should not be confused with "assisted living communities" that provide nursing and medical care. Assisted living communities generally are privately owned and operated by a corporate entity. They are considered a medical facility rather than a community association.

Some active adult communities have facilities for assisted living that are leased and operated by private care companies. Although they may be on property owned by the association or its members in undivided interest, the care facilities are not the responsibility of the community association.

The difference between active adult and assisted living communities may be confusing or difficult to understand, but they reflect a very important difference: Active adult communities are governed by a volunteer board elected by the members. Assisted living communities are operated by private entities like other commercial businesses.

Active adult communities can be any type of community association discussed in this book, although they often are assumed to be large Planned Unit Developments comprising single-family homes. This is the model used by Del Webb Developments for its famous Sun City communities. Other models are available, but many developers have copied that one with varying degrees of success.

To be considered an active adult community, a development simply must meet the age restrictions cited above and offer amenities and designs that attract the targeted buyers in a given market. As more people remain active longer, the demand for this kind of community association will increase, as will the pressure to cater to their interests and needs.

Many "fifty-five and older" communities, for example, have extensive outdoor amenities such as golf courses; lakes; multiple pools; tennis courts; bocce ball courts; shuffleboard courts; and parks with extensive BBQ facilities, picnic areas, and athletic fields. It also is common to find large community centers that house libraries; commercial-size kitchens for member parties; theaters with stage lighting for the presentation of plays, movies, and even talent shows; large areas for guest parking; outdoor entertainment areas; fitness centers that include salons, spas, and saunas; and even in-house restaurants and dining facilities.

Many of these communities even feature transportation systems to carry members to shopping malls and special entertainment and concert events in nearby neighborhoods, cities, and towns. In short, the list is limited only by the imagination and the members' ability and desire to pay.

Of course, one of the primary goals of most retirees is to control expenses. The challenge then becomes how to deliver all of these amenities and services within the financial parameters that must be met by the members. It is a challenge that the industry has not been able to answer completely—yet. Success requires understanding the diversity within the active adult population and adapting to it.

UNDERSTANDING THE
IMPACT OF BABY BOOMERS

To understand the scope of the changes necessary for the new American community to adapt to the new age demographic, it is useful to examine the root of the changes and the size of the approaching demographic wave.

Immediately following World War II there was a pronounced increase in the birth rate in the United States. This was due in part to the return of American GIs who, after the traumas of war, seemed to have a desire to settle down and start families. Coupled with the availability of jobs and relatively inexpensive housing in the suburbs, families began to grow.

A common expression of that era, based loosely on census data, was that the average American family comprised a mother, a father, 2.5 children, a dog, and a cat. While only an idiom, the statement was based on the reality of most American families. The population swelled from 175 million in the mid-1950s to 200 million in the late-1960s. The 2010 U.S. Census, by comparison, reports an estimated population of 300 million.

Based on related census data, the U.S. Administration on Aging (AoA) illustrated the rapid rate at which baby boomers are becoming golden boomers. This means they are reaching the once-traditional age of retirement, sixty-five:

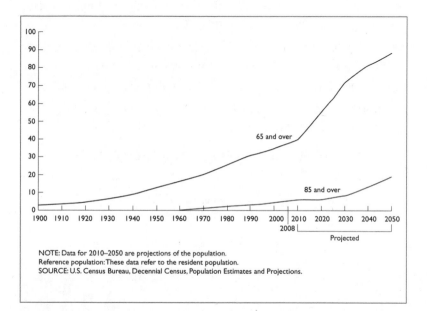

NOTE: Data for 2010–2050 are projections of the population.
Reference population: These data refer to the resident population.
SOURCE: U.S. Census Bureau, Decennial Census, Population Estimates and Projections.

The agency's chart indicates that the number of retirees reached approximately 40 million in 2010 and will reach almost 60 million in 2020. What's more, the average life expectancy continues to increase as more and more people remain healthy and active deep into their retirement years.

The effects of this aging population on the housing and community association industry are obvious. More and more developers are building communities to meet the needs of this growing population segment. In fact, the growth in the number and size of communities catering to persons fifty-five years and older is remarkable, especially in Sunbelt states such as Arizona and Florida, which traditionally are among the top choices of retirees.

AoA used census data to develop the following chart that illustrates the increase in the percentage of the population aged sixty and older, sixty-five and older, and eighty-five and older between 1900 and 2050: The percent of the population sixty and older grew from 6 percent in 1900 to 16 percent in 2000 and is projected to be 25 percent in 2030 and 26 percent in 2050. The percent of the population sixty-five and older increased from 4 percent in 1900 to 12 percent in 2000 and is projected to be 19 percent in 2030 and 20 percent in 2050. Finally, the percent of the population eighty-five and older expanded from 0.2 percent in 1900 to 1.5 percent in 2000 and is projected to be 2.3 percent in 2030 and 4.3 percent in 2050.

Older Population as a Percentage of the Total Population: 1900 to 2050

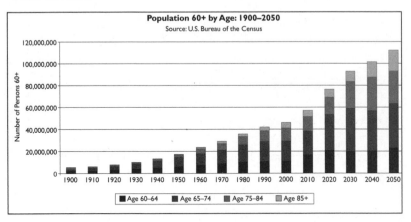

Sources:

Figures for projections from 2010 through 2050 are from Table 12, Projections of the Population by Age and Sex for the United States 2010 to 2050 (NP2008-T12), United States: 2010 to 2050 (NP2008-T12), Population Division, U.S. Census Bureau; Release Date: August 14, 2008. The data for 1900 through 2000 are from Appendix Table 5, Census 2000 Special Reports, Series CENSR-4, Demographic Trends in the 20th Century, 2002.

These data memorialize the baby boomer effect. They reinforce the notion that the population of the United States will age significantly in the next few decades. Simultaneously, they signal housing developers and managers to be sensitive to the demands of the emerging aging population who live or will live in community associations.

PROJECTING THE IMPACT OF RETIREES

The rate at which Americans are passing the retirement threshold is staggering. According to the American Association of Retired Persons (AARP), every day 10,000 Americans reach the once-traditional retirement age of sixty-five, and the pace is expected to continue for approximately twenty years. That is almost 80 million people or, according to the 2010 Census, slightly more than 26 percent of the population of the United States.

Because the U.S. Congress raised the age at which retirees can receive full social security retirement benefits, Americans who are older are expected to remain in the workforce until they are sixty-six or sixty-seven, depending on their age cohort. Many will stay in their homes longer, while others may never leave them.

Interestingly, the majority of baby boomers are expected to "retire in place," rather than relocate. In other words, they will retire in their current cities, towns, and residences and plan to live there as long as they are physically and mentally capable of doing so.

Sometimes this is an emotional choice based on comfort and familiarity. Other times the choice is based on economic limitations. Limited income, a house that already is paid for, and familiarity with local surroundings may all contribute to a person's "retire in place" decision, regardless of climate and location.

Wherever they live, Americans who are older will impact not only their communities but also the outcome of elections at all levels of government. In an article in *Psychology Today* (September 2011), Ben Y. Hayden, PhD, described the situation as follows:

In the United States, where voting is optional, the people who vote get to influence the country's direction. And the groups who vote more reliably tend to get their interests served by the government. And in this country, that's the elderly. Americans over 60 years old are 15 percent more likely to be registered to vote than those between 18 to 30. And registration strongly predicts voting—90 percent of registered voters voted in 2008, and obviously none of the non-registered voters voted.

It is just as likely that homeowners in this age group will vote in elections for community association boards of directors. Indeed, they are a force to be reckoned with!

ANALYZING THE IMPACT OF ACTIVE ADULT COMMUNITIES

It is in this climate that municipalities, developers, and professional community association managers are working to serve the interests of an active yet aging population.

The community association industry, for example, is adapting to meet the needs of the increasing number of retirees by developing active adult communities. These are not assisted living communities, which are usually privately owned and operated. They are community associations that are governed by boards of volunteers elected by homeowners. Typically they are managed by a professional manager who specializes in active adult communities. Their impact is as likely to increase, as is their number.

Impact on municipalities

The most immediate impact of the development of active adult communities is the creation of jobs. New jobs are created in the municipality to service the needs of adults who are fifty-five and older. They will need service and gas for their automobiles; use public transportation; dine out semi-regularly; and will frequent dry cleaners, supermarkets, movies, and a host of other recreational sites to fill their time.

Jobs will be created within the community association, including landscape maintenance, amenity operators (especially golf courses, pool, lakes, and clubhouses), activities personnel, management and bookkeeping personnel, leisure services personnel (concierge, masseuse, etc.), drivers, and other specialized workers. Of course, in these communities an eye always must be kept on operating expenses, and that likely will be the determinant for the number and type of personnel and services delivered.

As from all other forms of community associations, municipalities benefit from the establishment of active adult communities. Specifically, they enjoy an enhanced tax base due to high density housing without the responsibility of maintaining the infrastructure or of providing basic services such as trash removal within the association. They also will reap the ancillary economic benefit of expanded consumerism.

Residents in active adult communities often spend a portion of their time volunteering for groups in their local community. Hospitals, shelters, schools, and similar groups provide outlets for adults who are older to get involved and become an active part of the municipality.

Lifestyle choices

As with all community association lifestyle choices, home buyers must consider multiple factors, including housing cost, location, monthly maintenance assessments, access to medical care, and other expenses. Coupled with sensitivity to operating costs, these factors contribute to decisions of developers to build large communities for this growing segment of the population. The theory, of course, is to spread the costs over the greatest number of people.

Many aspects of active adult communities appeal to retirees, especially as their work-related social networks begin to shrink. Living in an active adult community offers them opportunities for new friendships and social contacts built around shared personal interests.

A true sense of community tends to develop as a result of homeowners identifying with new friends and building new social networks. Experience dictates that an active adult community, almost more than any other type of community association, naturally develops the sense of "emotional equity" discussed in earlier chapters.

Climate, cost, proximity to family, social networking, leisure time, amenities, hobbies, and interests all contribute to the appeal of active adult communities. The choice of a condominium versus a single-family home in a planned development will take all of these and several other factors into consideration.

Condominiums, for example, also will offer amenities, but they will be different and likely less expensive to operate. They might include a gym, community room, indoor pool and/or seasonal outdoor pool, transportation, and activities concierge. Most active adults choose condominium communities because of the lack of maintenance responsibilities, location (often in a city), and access to public transportation and busy cultural and nightlife activities.

Day-to-day operations

As in all community associations, membership in the association is mandatory and automatic for all owners. The affairs of the association are governed by a board of volunteers elected from the membership. A large majority of active adult communities hire professional management to handle the administrative and day-to-day operations of the association. The manager also acts as the board's professional adviser in matters of policy, budgets and finance, and rules and covenant enforcement.

Whatever the type of active adult community association, it requires that the board and manager have specialized training and skills. Sensitivity to the needs of the community may be heightened because a vast majority of the members will be retired and have more time on their hands. Some may even be willing to share their specialized professional expertise to assist the board and manager.

Active adult communities typically have a greater number of committees and member-populated task forces focused on achieving one-of-a-kind assignments. They also tend to have a greater number of social clubs and activities, including groups such as book clubs; poker clubs; bridge clubs; chess clubs; croquet leagues; baseball, softball, and basketball teams; tennis leagues; drama clubs; etc. All are organized and supported by the association and its staff. Some even have travel groups and special interest clubs, such as adventure travel clubs and wilderness groups.

Most, if not all, active adult communities offer short courses galore. A community in Arizona, for example, offers space for classes that focus on computer skills, website design and construction, and using eBay and electronic readers. They sponsor aerobics, water aerobics, tennis classes, and a myriad of other activities for the members.

Other communities have facilities for music classes, golf lessons, photography, and film. The list is almost endless. In an active adult community, if you can imagine a legal interest you can probably pursue it.

All of the activities are either sponsored and paid for by the association or are offerings of private companies and individuals.

New interests

The need for active adult communities is based on the increasing number of persons reaching retirement age and becoming empty nesters while still being healthy and active. They are interested in activities that allow social contact and opportunities to meet and have friendships with people of similar ages and interests.

A generation ago retirement meant slowing down and having

more leisure time but with fewer leisure activities convenient to location and lifestyle. Today's active adult communities meet these new
interests. They provide both beautiful, convenient locations and serve
the myriad of interests required by most persons who are older than
fifty-five. For those who can afford to relocate either down the street
or across the country to pursue their lifestyle choices, these communities can be ideal.

The greatest growth in this market segment has been and likely
will continue to be warmer climates in the Sunbelt. Traditionally this
includes Arizona, Florida, and Southern California. The National
Association of Homebuilders, however, also expects growth along the
entire Gulf Coast region. Most active adult retirees seem to be seeking a friendly climate with affordable housing and proximity to both
natural and man-made outdoor amenities.

Health care

Many active adult communities today are affiliated with private
health care or companies that provide assisted living care. These private companies may lease or own a facility within the association,
but their operations are completely separate. The association is not
involved in the health care needs of the members. Instead, the members contract separately with the private entity for nursing services,
health monitoring, special nutritional needs, medication supervision,
and therapies of all kinds.

These "on property" facilities act as an adjunct in allowing couples
to live together as long as possible when only one needs assisted care.
A couple in their eighties, for example, live in the same community
association, though in different wings of a building. Because he suffers with Alzheimer's and other chronic ailments, he receives assisted
care, mostly at night. Perfectly healthy, energetic, and alert, she spends
the days with him, unless he goes out with friends and supporters

who are sensitive to his needs. They often entertain visitors in private dining rooms or outdoors.

The situation is ideal for them. They can enjoy wonderful meals with other residents and participate in a wide variety of activities ranging from exercise and art classes to movies and artistic performances.

Indeed, active adult communities offer many alternatives. Based on their records and the growing population that is aging, they are destined for continued success.

CONCLUSION

Of all the community association choices, probably none is based as much on lifestyle choice as the active adult community. Generally, Americans are healthier as they get older and have access to better health care than ever. In short, they are living and staying active longer than other generations.

After a lifetime of responsibility they are shedding the burdens of maintaining a house and lawn in favor of the more maintenance-free community association lifestyle. They are discovering more time to spend with friends and to pursue interests they might not have had time for when they were younger.

The active adult community association seems to create a sense of community almost effortlessly, probably because members seek that sense of community more than any other factor. The community association offers a perfect vehicle for them to get connected and stay connected with a community of their age-group peers who share similar interests.

A common misconception persists that younger people are not welcome in a fifty-five+ community. On the contrary, visitors to one of these communities likely will find the children and grandchildren of members joining them and their friends to enjoy the pools, tennis facilities, and other activities.

What's more, because typically only 80 percent of the units must be occupied by at least one member who is fifty-five years or older, 20 percent of the units can be owned by persons who are younger.

The perception of this category of community associations as being "rest homes" or a place for the stodgy and bedridden is inaccurate. This truly is a great representation of the "new American community" and is embraced enthusiastically by those who choose it.

DAVID AND SANDRA
realize their American dream

Myth: Community association living focuses on condominiums and single-family homes, mostly for single persons and young families.

Buster: Community associations offer a great variety of homes and neighborhoods to serve all segments of the population, including active adult communities for the growing aging population.

David and Sandra realized their ultimate American dream in an active adult community. They never imagined the term "empty nesters" would describe them, but the years flew by, and they found themselves staring down a harsh reality: The house was quiet.

Their children were grown up. With one still in college and a college graduate working in another city, the couple found themselves wondering what to do with the extra space in their home. David was retiring, and Sandra worked at home, so they could move anywhere.

They realized their needs now were so similar to what they needed and wanted as newlyweds: great amenities and little maintenance. At this stage in their lives, choosing a one-story home seemed more practical for their future golden years.

David's older sister and brother-in-law had recently moved into an active adult community and urged David and Sandra to join them. The slightly younger couple couldn't imagine, however, that a community designed for a certain age group would have all that they wanted.

After some research and a few visits and tours, David and Sandra discovered that they actually could access more amenities in an active adult community than outside of one. Picturing themselves growing old together among family and friends with similar needs and interests, they made their decision.

The home they ultimately chose was perfect for their early retirement and in a community with numerous ways to remain active. Within walking distance, they had access to clubhouses, a theater, swimming pools, lawn bowling greens, shuffleboard courts, fitness centers, an arts and crafts center, two garden centers, a golf course, a tennis complex, and an equestrian center. Daily classes, lectures, movies, social hours, shopping trips, spa days, and many other activities were available on demand.

What they loved most was their new one-story single-family home. It was not only beautiful but also complied fully with the American Disabilities Act. Guests in wheelchairs could feel right at home.

If and when necessary, they could sell their home and move into one of the association's condominiums, affording them even fewer maintenance responsibilities without moving away from their new friends and neighbors.

Equally important, the community contracted with a private provider who operated an assisted living facility on the grounds. In fact, one spouse could live in a condominium, while the other lived in the assisted living facility—in the same building! The couple could spend their days together at either place or in the common areas but spend time separately as needed, mostly at night.

David and Sandra were immensely relieved to find such a wonderful place to retire. Their emotional equity in this new American community reinforced their peace of mind. Together they had come full circle in realizing their American dream while knowing that they found the perfect place where they could grow old together.

FREQUENTLY ASKED QUESTIONS

Q1: If I choose to live in an active adult community and my adult children need to move in with me temporarily, will this be allowed?

A1: Yes. Typically only one household resident who is a member of the association needs to be fifty-five years of age or older. Check the governing documents of the community you are buying into just to be sure.

Q2: If my wife and I live in an active adult community and one of us becomes impaired because of illness, will that affect our membership?

A2: No. If, however, you are concerned about one of you needing medical support or nursing care, you may want to consider an active adult community that includes a privately owned facility to accommodate people who move into the assisted living phase of life.

Q3: I am sixty years old, but my wife is only fifty-one. Can we still buy a unit and be members of an active adult community? If I should, God forbid, pass away before she is fifty-five, will she need to sell and move?

A3: As long as one member of the household is at least fifty-five, you and your wife qualify. On the question of your predeceasing your wife, she would not need to sell your home and move. The exception would be, however, if 20 percent of the households in the community did not have a member who was fifty-five or older. Because of federal mandates, active adult communities must ensure that 80 percent of the households have at least one adult who is fifty-five or older.

If this is a concern, you should have your lawyer review the association's CC&Rs with you before you purchase a home in it. There might be exceptions that would allow your wife a grace period during which the percentages in question could change or she might reach the required age.

Q4: My husband is intensely enthusiastic about his hobby. The community we are considering doesn't seem to have a group that addresses his interest. Shall we keep looking?

A4: You can always continue to look, but if you find a community that otherwise meets your needs, you should ask the manager about the possibility of starting a new interest group. Even if it were not endorsed by the community, perhaps he could organize an independent group within the community.

Q5: We are on a fixed income and are concerned that monthly assessments could rise and we would be forced to sell and move. Is there any way we can guarantee this doesn't happen?

A5: There are no guarantees, but rest assured that many persons who live in active adult communities share your concern. Also bear in mind that members elect the board of directors that would have to approve any new or increased assessments. Those volunteers are members of the community and probably are in the same financial position.

Before you decide to buy a home in an active adult community, be sure to review all the financial materials, including those pertaining to the budget and reserve funds. If you become a member, you also should serve on committees that impact the board's financial decisions. Nothing is healthier for the membership of a community than for interested members to educate themselves about its operation and then join the effort to keep it focused and successful.

CONCLUSION

We are what we repeatedly do.
Excellence, then, is not an act, but a habit.

—ARISTOTLE

The initial success of community associations in the United States was due to the economic benefits reaped by developers and municipalities and to the affordable lifestyle enhancements they offered to home buyers. Their phenomenal continued growth, however, can be attributed to their success in meeting their primary economic and "community" goals for homeowners. Those goals include protecting and enhancing property values while nurturing emotional equity and building community spirit.

Community associations are and likely will continue to be the fastest-growing segment of the housing market in most American cities. Although their evolution includes criticism that sometimes may have been justified, negative experiences served as lessons learned.

If industry leaders were not committed to learning from mistakes and to improving their standard of services, why would more than 62 million persons live in more than 314,000 community associations? These 2011 figures from the CAI reflect a steady growth from 1970 and project an upward pattern in the future.

It is precisely because developers, managers, municipalities, and association board members have learned from the past that they have improved and excelled. What's more, home buyers and homeowners have learned, too. The mutual expectations, understanding, and responsibilities that bind these groups form the foundation from which community associations will enjoy continued success.

Their perspectives are or should be consistent with Aristotle's wise words about excellence as a habit, not an act: For community associations, excellence in performance and in customer service must be a lifestyle, a culture, a habit. Only by striving to excel daily—by excelling repeatedly—will developers, managers, and board members meet and perhaps surpass the expectations of homeowners.

The popularity of community associations among home buyers is made possible by the developers and builders who create them and the municipalities that often require them and always benefit from them. While the diversity of lifestyles, amenities, and neighborhoods may appeal to home buyers, it also offers cost-effective options to developers and increased tax revenue to municipalities.

Whether condominiums, planned unit developments, or stock cooperatives, community associations are characterized by mandatory membership, mutually binding documents, and lien-based assessments. They operate as a business, act as a mini-government, and promote community spirit—all for the purpose of protecting the value of individual units on behalf of members. In meeting these purposes they coexist with local governments and offer homeowners amenities and levels of service that they probably would not enjoy outside community associations.

Although they may be managed professionally, community associations are governed by volunteers who serve on boards of directors, often assisted by volunteers who serve on committees. Indeed, they are one of the purest forms of participatory democracy.

When homeowners balance their individual needs and priorities with those of others, they nurture the emotional equity that results in a sense of community. Those who choose to live in a community association can serve their economic self-interest while enjoying a better quality of life. That choice typically reflects an interest in pursuing the

American dream in the easiest, most cost-effective way that satisfies their needs immediately while safeguarding their future.

Because they are more accessible, today's community associations are exactly the opposite of being exclusionary. They are home to diverse populations, reflecting a myriad of personal backgrounds, incomes, and demographics. Those homeowners can choose their communities in configurations ranging from condominiums and single-family homes to mixed-use, cooperatives, resort, and more. What drives the diversity? Market demand that is based largely on age, family status, and economics.

Because homes usually are the biggest piece of their financial portfolios, homeowners prioritize and expect positive returns on their investments. Community associations strive to meet those interests by protecting their property values directly and by reinvesting in their neighborhoods.

While these economic benefits are far-reaching, they are buoyed by the diverse range of social and cultural activities offered in community associations. That diversity often creates housing demands in new settings, as evidenced by the growing interest in moving back to stylish downtown living in urban areas. It also reflects adaptation to technological advancements that have globalized the world and enable professionals to work remotely.

Community associations will continue to thrive because of their ability to adapt to changing expectations and demographics, coupled with continued interests in protecting property values while enjoying a better quality of life. This is substantiated by Zogby's 2009 poll indicating that 71 percent of homeowners in community associations reported a positive overall experience, while only 12 percent were negative.

This high regard for community associations underscores their ability to adapt to meet changing needs. Initially formed to provide affordable housing and to offset the dwindling availability of buildable land, their goals evolved for the better.

Today they also strive to bring people with similar interests together in neighborhoods, to maintain and enhance the value of homes and of their community, to provide shared amenities, to excel in customer service and member participation, and to accommodate the changing work and lifestyle demands of a modern society. As they evolve to meet those changing needs, community associations will continue to prosper.

Their prosperity will depend not only on protecting property values but also on fostering emotional equity among homeowners. Those who perceive the advantages of living in community associations often build their emotional equity on feeling safe and secure in their homes.

Community association board members are volunteers with limited experience in running multimillion-dollar not-for-profit associations and even less time to do so. Accordingly, an estimated 15–17 percent of community associations in the United States hire professional managers to help them make the best policy decisions.

Today's managers typically act as consultants to the board. They help board members improve their governance practices, policies, and procedures, especially by making wise decisions, responding effectively to negativity, being reasonable and flexible in implementing rules and in interacting with homeowners, and adapting to changing issues.

Well-run community associations become coveted in particular areas. Living in them is significantly different than the alternative. Their ability to provide privacy, independence, and a sense of community differentiates them from other types of housing options. As more home buyers learn about their advantages, the demand for community associations will increase, and they will continue to thrive.

Understanding how community associations work, why people prefer them, and why they will continue to thrive is the foundation from which to determine how to improve them. The answer is through education, performance, and adaptation to external forces.

Educating homeowners is critical so that they understand the mutual interests and responsibilities of living in community associations. This effort should begin with home buyers, who clearly must understand the governing documents and whether a particular association is suitable for their lifestyles.

Simultaneously, board members, Realtors®, managers, and other professionals must participate in continuing education activities that are designed to empower them to excel.

Community associations can improve their performance by developing the ability and extending the knowledge of board members; improving the efficiency, transparency, and productivity of board members while enhancing participation; and improving the measurements of success.

To measure success, for example, board members, managers, and homeowners need to be keenly aware of the association's viability in the market. They should understand the impact that rules and CC&Rs—and their enforcement—have on property values. Those values should be emphasized repeatedly in all communications from boards and managers. This will assure homeowners that the board is aware of and continually focused on issues that affect the members and their assets.

Internal efforts to improve community associations, however, must be coupled with efforts to adapt to external forces, including the priorities of developers, changes in technology and media, and the effects of legislation.

Developers are absolutely critical to the continued success and improvement of community associations. The best developers today learned from the shoddy construction and lawsuits of the past and strive to offer better products. The countless opportunities they have at hand include developing reader-friendly governing documents that are reasonable and fair; embracing long-term, sound budgeting practices; employing high-quality professionals; ensuring an effective board of directors; providing ongoing training for and establishing strong relationships with homeowners, board members, and personnel; and providing sustainable and green communities.

Changes in technology are another important avenue for

improvement. Community associations and management firms will need to be reactive by keeping up with the changes but also proactive by embracing innovation and shaping customers' expectations. To remain competitive, for example, they must adopt the technology and information standards of advanced industries that offer 24/7 access to information exchanges in real time.

Technological advancements also can improve board meetings and promote homeowners' participation, especially by broadcasting meetings online or via closed circuit television and posting meeting materials online. Equally if not more important, they are tools for achieving peace of mind. The most obvious examples of using technology to enhance security are digital cameras that provide visual coverage of common areas, and eye and face recognition for entry into homeowner units and common areas.

Community associations also can improve by adapting to the changes in the media landscape. They can reach home buyers and homeowners simultaneously and economically via digital media. By employing websites and a rich variety of social channels and other online media, they can tell their story and help resolve problems when they occur.

Changes in legislation are another external force that impact the improvement of community associations. Instead of simply reacting to the actions of elected bodies at the local, state, and federal levels, they should get involved early in the process and stay involved at all stages.

Typically because of misunderstandings about modern community association practices, critics sometimes propose legislation that can be detrimental to homeowners. Legislative micromanaging or a negligent board can undermine the process of board members who can make decisions required to preserve and enhance association property values.

To adapt to a period of greater government scrutiny and regulation, community associations should set a positive agenda that empowers homeowners and not government. They are more likely to thrive if they stay abreast of legal requirements and speak out to ensure that policy makers can make informed decisions. The key to the future vibrancy of community associations is for homeowners to engage in the governance and legislative process.

Interestingly, community associations are evolving not only in the United States but also throughout the world. Their diversity is reflected in the time-share vacation resorts in Mexico; condominiums in Canada; high-density affordable housing in South America; multi-unit housing in the form of apartments or flats in Europe; exclusive mixed-use, high-rise associations in Dubai and other parts of the Middle East; high-rise, multifamily residential communities in Asia and South Africa; and a range from high-rise beachfront communities to quiet residential enclaves in Australia.

Indeed, community associations are a worldwide phenomenon. All share the common goal of protecting property values while offering shared amenities and a better quality of life.

In preparing for the future, community associations in the United States must continue to meet the needs and demands of their changing markets. This means adapting their goals, marketing, and customer service based on the multicultural aspects of the country's changing demographics.

The 2010 Census, for example, projects a population of up to 458 million inhabitants by 2050—138 million more than the 320 million counted in 2010. That population is expected to be not only older and more racially and ethnically diverse but also amiable and accepting of increased diversity.

How can developers, board members, and managers succeed in the future without understanding how their markets are changing? Their bottom line can be impacted negatively if they ignore or fail to appreciate multicultural diversity and differences. Understanding their impact, however, can facilitate success, particularly in attracting home buyers and retaining homeowners.

Dealing with multiculturalism and diversity includes overcoming cultural barriers and avoiding gaffes in language and behavior. It requires specific action steps, including analyzing the customer base, researching the market and potential home buyers, identifying ways to reach out and engage persons from identified cultures and demographic groups, planning appropriate diversity training, adapting marketing strategies, and developing multicultural customer service strategies—and continued training.

Taking those steps will enable community associations to enhance their success and to reap the benefits of dealing effectively with the changing demographics.

A special effort, however, must be made to meet the needs of the aging population, especially as the "baby boomers" become "golden boomers." One of every five Americans will be older than sixty-five by 2031, according to the National Association of Area Agencies on Aging.

Clearly, there is an increasing need for active adult communities for residents who are fifty-five years and older. By offering the appropriate amenities and governing documents, these community associations can meet the needs of this growing and important segment of our population.

Based on their history, community associations will adapt successfully not only to the aging and increasingly diverse population but also to the changing market demand. This will require their continued commitment to learning from justifiable criticism, listening to homeowners, educating stakeholders, being reasonable and fair, improving their products and services, and preparing for the future.

Readers of this book probably are a part of the community association family and can make a difference in securing a bright future. Their children, grandchildren, and future generations will create neighborhood memories based on their mutual experiences in a community association. The powerful legacy they will inherit will enable them to continually improve the quality of life provided therein.

May they embrace the many opportunities and benefits described herein and, together, in the common interest, continue to embrace the new American community.

ACKNOWLEDGMENTS

Writing a book can never be accomplished without the help of a lot of people. First and foremost I thank my wife, Helen. As my best friend and colleague she has encouraged me for years to undertake this journey. Equally supportive and encouraging were my three oldest sons, Joey, Jeff, and Will, who also join me in the community association management industry, namely. Our younger children, Kirsten and Kellen, embrace our commitment to our extended Associa family. All of us believe strongly in the importance of implementing family values in the workplace.

Many of my Associa staff also contributed to the process. Especially noteworthy and deeply appreciated were the significant collaboration and contributions of Matt Kraft, Larry Pothast, Lauren Anderson, Andrew Fortin, Barbara Herndon, Craig Koss, Bill Maselunas, Mike Packard, Carol Piering, Michael Robinson, Todd Strosnider, Debra Warren, Angela Frieling, and Christy Earl. Thanks to all of them for making my job easier—not only in this endeavor, but also every day.

I am especially appreciative of the community association management industry. Developers and members of the associations that we manage continuously challenge us to improve and to adapt our service to meet their changing needs. Our management team inspires us to excel, and our vendors are important partners in this process.

We have learned valuable lessons from them, as we have from our competitors and even from our critics. As service providers we welcome opportunities to build upon our successes and to respond swiftly and appropriately to criticism. This facilitates our improvement, strengthens our performance, and stimulates our growth. For this, we are grateful.

Finally, I thank our partners throughout the world—everyone responsible for the growth of community associations in the United States and beyond. Whatever their purpose and role and however it may differ from ours, we share a vision for improving the quality of life of the homeowners we serve.

GLOSSARY

The Community Association Institute has an excellent glossary of terminology frequently used in the community association management industry. Although subject to change, the link to its website is provided below. It is used herein with permission from the Foundation for Community Association Research (*www.cairf.org*).

http://www.artisanelearning.com/clients/CAI/Glossary_3-17 /engage.html

This glossary is a work in progress. To contribute terms, definitions, or feedback, please email Dave Jennings, vice president for education, via djennings@caionline.org.

SELECTED REFERENCES

Chapter 1

Community Associations Institute. www.caionline.org.

Chapter 2

Rathburn, Frank, ed. *Industry Data*. Community Associations Institute. Sept. 27, 2012. <http://www.caionline.org/info/research/Pages/default.aspx>.

US Census Bureau. *1970 Census of Population and Housing*. Sept. 27, 2012. <http://www.census.gov/prod/www/abs/decennial/1970.html>.

US Census Bureau. *2010 Census*. Sept. 27, 2012. <http://2010.census .gov/2010census/data/>.

Chapter 3

Research Foundation of the Community Associations Institute. Zogby Polls, 2005, 2007, and 2009.

2010 U.S. Census. www.census.gov.

Research Foundation of the Community Associations Institute. Zogby Poll, 2009.

Chapter 4

Hyatt, Wayne S. Putting the Community Back in Community Associations: An Action Plan. In *Community First!: Emerging visions reshaping America's condominium and homeowner associations*, edited by Bill Overton. Alexandria, VA: Community Associations Press, 1999.

Vance, Mike. Disney University and the Creative Thinking Institute.

Chapter 5

O'Connor, Michol. *O'Connor's Texas Causes of Action*. Houston: Jones McClure Publishing, 2012.

Robert, Henry Martyn. *Robert's Rules of Order Newly Revised*. 11th ed. Revised and edited by the Council of the Robert's Rules Association Authorship Team. Boston and New York: Da Capo Press, 2011.

Chapter 6

Federal Communications Commission. *The Information Needs of Communities*. 2011.

Agan, Amanda and Alexander Tabarrok. "Do Homeowners Associations Raise Property Values? What are Private Governments Worth?" *Regulation*. Fall 2005, p. 17.

Research Foundation of the Community Associations Institute. Zogby poll.

Approval Provisions for the Federal Housing Administration (FHA) Condominium Approval Process, Section 2.1.5, page 7 (2012).

North Carolina General Statutes, Chapter 47, Section 47F-3-116-(a).

Some of the best blogs and websites about association living are listed below:

› Association Times www.associationtimes.com

› HOA Management Blog http://www.hoamanagementblog.com/

› Condo Association Management Blog http://www.condoassociation.com/blog/
   HOA Management Directory Blog http://www.hoamanagementdirectory.com/blog.html

› Condo and HOA Law Blog http://CondoandHOALawBlog.com

Many state legislatures host great online resources. Texas' website, for example, allows stakeholders to register for alerts about legislative action related to selected issues, to search specific topics, and to track bills of interest. Some of the major state sites are listed below:

› Arizona: http://www.azleg.gov/

› California: http://www.legislature.ca.gov/

> Florida: http://www.myfloridahouse.gov/

> Texas: http://www.capitol.state.tx.us/

Chapter 7

Foroohar, Rana. The World's Best Countries. *Newsweek*. 2010. http://www.thedailybeast.com/newsweek/2010/08/16/best-countries-in-the-world.html.

Wikipedia–The Free Encyclopedia, Condominium–Canada. Accessed August 18, 2012.

http://en.wikipedia.org/wiki/Condominium#Canada.

The Canadian Condominium Institute (CCI). About CCI. Accessed August 19, 2012.

http://www.cci.ca/ABOUT/whoweare.asp.

The Association of Condominium Managers of Ontario (ACMO), About Us. Accessed August 15, 2012. http://www.acmo.org/acmo.php?id=1.

The Association of Condominium Managers of Alberta (ACMA). Accessed August 15, 2012. http://www.myacma.com/.

Wikipedia–The Free Encyclopedia, Timeshare. Accessed August 20, 2012.

http://en.wikipedia.org/wiki/Timeshare.

RCI®. About Us accessed August 17, 2012. http://www.rci.com/RCI/RCIW/RCIW_index?body=RCIW_AboutUs.

Interval International. Accessed August 17, 2012. http://www.intervalworld.com/web/my/home.

Wikipedia–The Free Encyclopedia. Brazil. Accessed August 18, 2012; http://en.wikipedia.org/wiki/Brazil.

Wikipedia–The Free Encyclopedia. Condominiums UK and Norway. Accessed August 16, 2012.

http://en.wikipedia.org/wiki/Condominiums#England_and_Wales_2C_UK.

U.S. Central Intelligence Agency. The World Factbook. Accessed August 15, 2012.

www.cia.gov/library/publications/the-world-factbook.

Dubai Real Estate Institute (DREI). Accessed August 16, 2012. http://www.drei.ae/.

Wikipedia–The Free Encyclopedia. Condominium – Singapore/Shanghai. Accessed August 18, 2012. http://en.wikipedia.org/wiki/Condominium#Singapore.

U.S. Central Intelligence Agency. The World Factbook. Accessed August 15, 2012.

www.cia.gov/library/publications/the-world-factbook.

Chapter 8

U.S. Census Bureau. 2010 Census. www.census.gov.

U.S. Equal Employment Opportunity Commission. http://www.eeoc.gov/.

Chapter 9

U.S. Census Bureau. 2010 Census. www.census.gov.

The National Association of Area Agencies on Aging (N4A). www.n4a.org.

U.S. Social Security Administration. www.ssa.gov.

U.S. Administration on Aging. (table). www.aoa.gov. Source cited: U.S. Census Bureau. Decennial Census. Population Estimates and Projections.

American Association of Retired Persons. www.aarp.org.

Hayden, Ben Y. "Why Do Older People Vote More?" *Psychology Today*. September 2011.

INDEX

ABOUT THE AUTHOR

JOHN CARONA is the founder, president, and chief executive officer of Associa, the nation's largest community association management firm. His experience and expertise encompass all aspects of residential real estate, including the development, leasing, management, and maintenance of single and multifamily communities. A Professional Community Association Manager, Carona also is licensed as a Real Estate Broker in Texas. Under his direction, Associa has grown during a period of enormous change and is recognized as the industry's leading innovator.

Also an accomplished legislator, Carona has served five terms in the Texas Senate and three in the Texas House of Representatives. His statewide legislative leadership roles include serving as Chairman of the Senate Transportation and Homeland Security Committee and Chairman of the Senate Business and Commerce Committee. A variety of organizations have honored him for his dedication to pressing issues, including public education, criminal justice, and economic development. He was named the "Champion of Free Enterprise," three times a "Crime Fighter of the Year," the "Most Valuable Player–Texas Senate," and twice as one of the "Ten Best Legislators" by *Texas Monthly* magazine.

While running a thriving international business and authoring or serving as chief sponsor of more than five hundred bills that became law, John remains family focused. He lives in Dallas with his wife, Helen, and is the father of five children and the grandfather of five more. A graduate of The University of Texas at Austin, he holds a bachelor of business administration degree in insurance and real estate. An avid art collector, he enjoys traveling with his family, ranching, and hunting.